YONANAS

FROZENHEALTHYDESSERT MAKER® COOKBOOK

121 EASY & UNIQUE FROZEN TREATS AND ALCOHOLIC DESSERTS (INCLUDING NON-DESSERT RECIPES LIKE MASHED POTATOES, HUMMUS AND GUACAMOLE!)

Vanessa Blanc

Yonanas Frozen Healthy Dessert Maker® Cookbook

TABLE OF CONTENTS

Gentle Reminder:

Remember: this book is not a replacement for your Yonanas Healthy Dessert Maker®'s User Guide. Please check the literature provided by the manufacturer before using this machine.

WHY CHOOSE A YONANAS FROZEN HEALTHY DESSERT MAKER®?

Everything these days is on a fast-track. We want convenient, quick and easy. Fast food, grocery delivery service, overnight shipping. We want what we want, and we want it *now*.

Sure, ice cream makers and food processors have a place in our kitchen, but sometimes the time just doesn't exist for multi-step, long process recipes. Get a Yonanas Healthy Dessert Maker® and get instant dessert.

It's light weight, all-in-one-piece model, makes it super easy to store, clean and travel with. Everything can be attached, which means no loose pieces will be falling all over the place when it's pulled out of storage or off the shelf. The important parts are all dishwasher safe, so only limited scrubbing is required. Make dessert and instantly enjoy it instead of spending time cleaning up and staring at the clock waiting for the moment it's finally frozen enough to eat.

Enjoy instant ice creams and sorbets, frozen cakes, pies and popsicles, and even some non-dessert dishes like hummus and mashed potatoes.

How it works
Easy Peasy.
1. All you do is feed frozen fruit, and other ingredients of your choice, into the chute.
2. Turn on the machine and press down with the plastic plunger when the chute is full.
3. Out comes a creamy frozen treat. Instant ice creams and frozen yogurt.

How it compares to other machines

With the market as saturated with blenders and ice cream makers, it can be hard to make a decision about which product to purchase. Educating yourself about other products and how they stack up against the Yonanas Healthy Dessert Maker® is the best solution.

Ice Cream Makers

Perfect for making ice cream. This may seem obvious, but this is exactly what small appliances like the Cuisinart ICE-100 were created to do. Making your ice cream at home can be beneficial since you can control the ingredients. You can control dietary restrictions like dairy and opt for almond or coconut milk, and you can cut back on the amount of sugar that goes into your dessert. Some ice cream makers are 100% automatic and come with self-freezing bowls, yielding instant gratification with ready to eat ice cream. However, ice cream makers come at a cost. Most of these appliances pack quite a punch to your pocket book and are incredibly difficult to clean and maintain.

Frozen Dessert Makers

There are a few brands of dessert makers similar to the Yonanas Healthy Dessert Maker®. The Magic Dessert Bullet® and Big Boss Swirlo® are the most comparable. But what is the real difference in the brands? Not much. Power and dimensions are the biggest difference on paper. The Magic Bullet is the winner when it comes to power. With 350 Watts it is the most powerful of the three, followed by the Yonanas Healthy Dessert Maker® with 200 Watts and the Big Boss Swirlo® with only 130 Watts. Why is this important? Because when grinding up frozen fruit you want the machine to be able to handle it without shutting down. The dimensions also vary just slightly. For the most part, the machines look similar, all have plungers and chutes, are made of plastic, BPA-free, and dishwasher safe. While the function of a particular device might suit you better, this is something you won't know until you've purchased one and tried it out. The Yonanas Healthy Dessert Maker® is currently the most expensive, followed by the Magic Bullet Dessert Bullet® and the Big Boss Swirlo®.

Pros & Cons

We consider the Yonanas Healthy Dessert Maker® to be a fantastic choice for your household frozen dessert appliance. We want you to weigh all your options. Make informed decisions. Here are some Pros and Cons of the machine.

Pros

Healthy-Frozen fruits make this a healthy option. Less sugar and dairy-free, if you want. You choose your ingredients. You control what goes into the machine. There are so many options, both healthy and not so healthy. The ingredients and combinations are endless.

Super easy to use-Fill the chute, press down on the plastic plunger to send ingredients through the chute and enjoy. It is that easy. 1-2-3.

Multipurpose-Dishwasher safe- Even though you have to take apart and rinse the individual pieces you can quickly pop them into the dishwasher.

Lightweight-The machine itself is super lightweight and very easy to move around. You can take it to a friend's house or an event so easily.

It's fun to experiment-This is the number one reason to purchase the Yonanas Healthy Dessert Maker®. It's fun. The possibilities are endless. You can just toss in whatever sweet treats you have lying around your home and have an instant creamy dessert.

Noisy- While this machine is not much stronger than a blender, many users have mentioned that it is really loud. The Yonanas *Elite* Frozen Healthy Dessert Maker® is said to be a bit quieter.

Not a breeze to clean-Dishwasher safe doesn't mean just pop the whole thing into the dishwasher. Frozen fruits can be tricky and get sticky if not rinsed right away. Unscrewing the parts and rinsing them under warm water or soaking them for a while can help cut back on the cleaning issues many users complain about.

Letting the fruit thaw-The guide book suggests letting the frozen fruit sit on the counter for about 5 – 10 minutes. But waiting that extra time can be hard to do. When you want ice cream, you want it right then. But if the fruit doesn't thaw the texture is very gritty and not as creamy as it should be. So, take a pause for the cause and wait that extra few minutes.

Difficult to make large quantities-It could take a while if you're trying to feed a bunch of people, and by the time you've popped out 4 bowls the first bowl is well on its way to fully melted.

A lot of leftovers caught inside the machine-This can be wasteful, not to mention the amount of ingredients it can take to create one actual serving.

GETTING TO KNOW YOUR YONANAS HEALTHY DESSER MAKER®

For foodies, appliances can turn out to be best friends or enemies. They're very much like people. The more you get to know your device the more likely you are to fall in love with it and the more you want to see it, spend time with it, do new and exciting things with it. So get to know how your Yonanas Healthy Dessert Maker®. I guarantee you will be delighted when you discover all the awesome it has to offer.

YONANAS HEALTHY DESSERT MAKER® ACCESSORIES INCLUDED

Here's what comes in the box. Make sure it's all here before you start making treats.

Base: this is the heart and soul of the machine. It houses the motor and has an electrical cord.

Chute: this is where all the ingredients are inserted. It also covers the blade.

Plunger: used to press down the food when the chute gets full.

Blade Cone: the actual blade.

Gasket: plastic that goes under the blade to prevent leakage.

Bottom cap: screws everything together and makes the machine one, nice, connected piece of equipment.

OTHER ACCESSORIES NO INCLUDED

Pie pan: pie and cake recipes call for a pie pan, so if you don't have one pick one up. 9-inch.

Popsicle trays: You can make your own with Dixie cups and popsicle sticks, but it is much easier to purchase some inexpensive plastic ones that can be reused. Buy different sizes yielding a different number of servings. You never know how many people you will be feeding with your popsicles.

Ice cube trays: Some recipes will make cute little bite sized treats. Ice cube trays are used to freeze them in, so mix it up and try some fun shapes.

Small mixing bowls: Having all your ingredients lined up and ready to go is a must. The machine moves quickly, so have some small bowls available will all your ingredients measured out.

Stainless steel bowls: Some recipes call for stainless steel bowls for easy heating. You will need this if you choose to try those recipes. There is no acceptable substitute.

Measuring cups and spoons: Everything is measured out. So while this is not an exact science, you will want to get in the general area of correct measurements.

Assembly
1.Remove all parts from the plastic.
2. Insert the rubber gasket into the hard-plastic bottom cap. Be sure to put the bottom part of the gasket (larger part) into the top part of the cap.
3. The blade cone fits on top of the gasket, making one piece.
4. Screw the one piece into the plastic chute. The bottom cap and chute will screw together, but be sure it is evenly in place. This will also create one piece.
5. Take the cute and fit it into the machine base. Turn counterclockwise until it clicks.
You should have one piece with no loose parts.

HOW TO ADJUST RECIPES FOR THE YONANAS HEALTHY DESSERT MAKER®

You can adjust almost any frozen dessert recipe to fit your Yonanas Healthy Dessert Maker®. Whether it's ice cream, healthy dessert, frozen fruit treats, frozen yogurt, popsicles, or even frozen pies and cakes you're after, this little machine can do it all. There are just a few things to keep in mind when converting recipes.

Liquids

Limit the amount of liquid you use. The chute is open straight through, from top to bottom. The Yonanas Healthy Dessert Maker® is not a juicer, so if you put in a liquid by itself, it will run right out. Try mixing the liquids with other ingredients and alternate adding ingredients. Add some solids before and after the fluids. If it is necessary to use liquids, try freezing it for a little bit until it becomes slushy. Everything comes out super creamy so you shouldn't need a whole lot of liquid anyways.

Timing

Most of the actual work is just running ingredients through the chute. This is a quick process, usually only taking a few minutes. It goes very quickly so be sure to have everything you need set out in bowls, so you don't have to scramble to feed in the next ingredient. Soft serve, frozen yogurt, and ice cream take only minutes to complete but keep in mind that if you are making popsicles or frozen desserts like cakes and pies you will still need to budget 3-4 hours of freeze time.

Do not use ice

While it is okay to use frozen ingredients, like fruit or juice concentrate, it is never okay to use ice. The chute is relatively small, and the blades are shaped and housed differently than a blender or food processor. If you need to pre-freeze ingredients like milk or yogurt, just be sure it is only frozen to a slushy consistency and not rock hard. Using ice or other extremely hard, frozen solids will likely damage your machine.

Non-dessert recipes

When making non-dessert recipes like hummus or mashed potatoes be sure that your ingredients are **_always_** precooked. Nothing raw, especially eggs. Since you won't be using frozen fruits, your ingredients like potatoes should be boiled, not too soft, though, and slightly cooled. You will need something solid, but not too hard, that can be easily pushed through the chute and made into a creamy texture. You will be a Yonanas expert soon, so apply all the same rules, like alternating ingredients and limiting your liquids, to your non-dessert recipes.

HOW TO OPERATE YOUR YONANAS HEALTHY DESSER MAKER®

Your Yonanas Healthy Dessert Maker® is super easy to use. Every recipe, no matter what the ingredients, follows the same steps.

1.Set out all ingredients. The machine moves fast, so be sure to have all your ingredients measured out and into bowls for a smooth process.

2. Place a bowl under the chute to catch all your treats.

3. Turn on the machine.

4. Alternate adding ingredients to the chute until it is full. Make sure to sandwich liquids in between solids, so they don't run straight through the chute.

5. Press down with the plastic plunger, pushing ingredients through the chute.

6. Repeat steps 4 and 5 until all ingredients are used.

Minutes later you will have a delicious treat to enjoy. Be sure to completely disassembled and clean the appliance after each use.

HOW TO STORE YOUR TREATS

If you have a crazy amount of self-control and don't enjoy your frozen snacks immediately after making them, we envy you. Treats can usually be stored up to 2 or 3 weeks in the freezer. You can purchase freezer bags or use containers.

Freezer bags

Be sure your baggies are "freezer" baggies. This seems obvious but is often accidently overlooked, and no one likes freezer burn. If you choose to use to use freezer bags all you need to do is toss your treats inside and zip it up. Make sure they are completely frozen, so they don't stick together.

Storage Containers

You can also use containers to store your treats. Be sure to layer with parchment paper, so they don't stick together. Items stored in containers are usually more tightly packed than when stored in freezer bags and sometimes get stuck together.

CLEANING AND DISASSEMBLING YOUR YONANAS HEALTHY DESSERT MAKER®

So now you have a fabulous frozen dessert to enjoy, but don't forget to clean your machine immediately. If you don't have time to clean it right away, at least rinse it under some warm water. This helps all the fruit to wash off and makes for an easier clean up later. Rinsing helps to prevent fruit from sticking and any future scrubbing.

1.Turn the chute clockwise until it comes loose.
2. Remove the plunger from the chute.
3. Unscrew the bottom cap and blade cone. Be careful as the blade is sharp!
4. Separate the rubber gasket, bottom cap, and blade cone.
5. Rinse all pieces, except the base, under warm water. You can use a scrub brush to remove particles stuck in the blades or corners of the gasket and bottom cap.
6. Wipe down the base with a damp cloth. DO NOT RINSE OR SUBMERGE IN WATER. The base has an electrical cord. It should never be submerged in water.
7. Put all parts, not the base, into the dishwasher.

You're ready for more Yonanas fun!

TOPPING/ADDITIVES GUIDE

Nut Butters

Nut butters are always a nice flavor that can be added to many frozen treats. They can be used a couple ways. First, you can run a few tablespoons through the Yonanas Healthy Dessert Maker® along with the other ingredients. This will help to blend well with the other ingredients and give more of an overall flavor. Be sure to not add more than 3 tablespoons as it could clog up the chute and blades. You can also hand swirl the nut butter in after. Just dollop the butter into the frozen treats and swirl with a spoon. This option gives a burst of flavor. Some great options would be apple butter, peanut butter, almond butter, or Nutella.

Milk

When adding milk, it is crucial not to use too much. A few tablespoons can go a long way add flavor and a creamy texture. Unless the recipe calls for more, 2 tablespoons are usually enough. Liquid runs right through the chute, so be sure to put a solid in first. You can always partially freeze the milk to create a slushy texture. This will help keep the liquid from running out. Besides obvious dairy milk, try almond milk, soy milk or coconut milk. They come in all kinds of flavors like vanilla, chocolate or strawberry, and be purchased sweetened or unsweetened.

Yogurt

Yogurt can be fun. Many recipes already call for its use, but don't feel like you need to use the flavor the recipe calls for. With so many different brands and so many different flavors, there is no reason not to experiment. Since yogurt is a soft solid, it can be added to the machine as-is with ease, but try freezing it in mini-ice cube trays or in spoonfuls on parchment paper. The frozen servings will be even easier to plunge into the machine with the frozen fruit. Greek yogurt will yield a thicker texture than regular yogurt, but it will also have more of a bite to it. If you are trying to be dairy-free, opt for a coconut yogurt. They have Greek coconut yogurt and regular coconut yogurt as well.

Candy

Endless. Possibilities. Seriously. So while "healthy" is in the Yonanas name, you can still add candy. Just do it. You know you want to. Take your favorite candy and either add it to the machine during the feeding process or use it as a garnish afterward. Most chocolate candy, like Snickers, Twix, Hershey's bars, or chocolate chips can be added to the chute in small pieces without issue. Gummi candies and hard candy should be used strictly as a garnish. The gummi texture is liable to clog up the blades, and hard candy will likely just break your machine altogether.

Fruits

Double up on the fruit action. Chop fruits, or use their natural juices, as garnishes. Fresh fruit would be a nice compliment to a frozen fruit treat.

Frinkles and Sprinkles

The little kid in all of us wants some sprinkles. So honor your inner child and give yourself a nice tablespoon of rainbow or chocolate sprinkles! Too much sugar for your taste? Yonanas makes little bags of awesome toppings called "Frinkles". These are freeze-dried fruits that look like sprinkles. They come in flavors like Berry Blast and Tropical Fruit.

Cookie Dough

Find some great cookie dough! Add it on top to any recipe for an added treat. Be sure to use vegan cookie dough, so you don't consume uncooked eggs.

Sauces

Sauce it up. Don't be afraid to add some strawberry, chocolate or caramel sauce to your frozen treats. You can add a tablespoon or 2 to the chute with the other ingredients for an overall flavor or drizzle some sauce on top of the finished product.

Soda

Have a float. Toss some ice cream or frozen bites in something carbonated. Don't stop at a root beer or coke float, but try other flavors like cream soda, sarsaparilla or something that will complement the flavor of your treat.

Nuts or Coconut Flakes

Garnish your fro-yo or ice cream with roasted, toasted or fresh nuts or flakes. Pistachios, almonds, cashews, walnuts, macadamia nuts, peanuts, or coconut are some great choices to sprinkle on top of any frozen dessert. It adds a new flavor and a different texture.

Cookies

Crumble your favorite cookie and add as a topping or add some during your creation process. Add some crunch to your creamy. Oreos, gingersnaps, vanilla wafers, and chocolate chip cookies are always great options, but we'll let you choose your favorite.

TEXTURE GUIDE

Not all frozen treats are created equal. Different desserts are made with different ingredients, thus yielding different textures and flavors. Here is a cheat sheet to help you decide which one suits you best.

Ice Cream

Cool and creamy, this dessert is usually made with milk. It also typically contains sugar or corn syrup for a very sweet flavor.

Sorbet

If fruit is your thing, then sorbet should be your go-to frozen treat. The texture is rough and somewhat icy, as sorbet is almost always dairy free. Flavors are refreshing and zestier tasting than creamy.

Sherbet

Not to get confused with sorbet, Sherbet typically contains dairy. The taste is similar to sorbet in that it is refreshing and fruity, but sherbet will have a creamier texture and flavor because of the dairy content. Keep in mind that nondairy milk will yield equally smooth results, so don't rule sherbet out completely if you're going for a dairy-free dessert.

Popsicle

Popsicles aren't always frozen, icy treats, some can have a fudgy or creamy texture. Most popsicles are frozen using popsicles trays with sticks, but popsicle bites are becoming a new trend. Using ice cube trays, with no sticks, popsicle recipes can be transformed into bite-sized treats in fun shapes. The bites are also easier to transport in baggies or containers.

Gelato

Rich. Decadent. Elegant. All words that accurately describe gelato. It is almost always higher in sugar and will have a softer texture as it does not freeze completely.

Frozen Yogurt

Made with.... you guessed it! Yogurt. Whether it is Greek yogurt, regular yogurt, low-fat, or coconut yogurt you can bet on yogurt being in your...well.... frozen yogurt. While sugar is sometimes added, this frozen treat has a little bit of a bite or hint of sour to it because yogurt is the main ingredient. Fruit and chocolate compliment almost any fro-yo flavor.

PANTRY STOCKING GUIDE

The possibilities with your Yonanas Healthy Dessert Maker® are virtually endless. The good news is that many recipes use the same, or similar, ingredients. You can always make ahead and freeze your treats.

Since many of these ingredients come frozen or are non-perishable, it makes sense to purchase them in bulk.

List of the most mentioned ingredients in this book. Use it as a guide for your shopping list.

Sugar: you can always use natural sweeteners, but if you choose to use sugar try to find a quick dissolve, super fine sugar. Regular sugar can also be run through a food processor to make it finer. It makes for a less grainy texture.

Honey, agave nectar or stevia: natural sweeteners are a go-to for healthy desserts. The taste isn't changed that much, and they are low-glycemic. The honey and nectar can also create a nice binding agent for some recipes.

Frozen Bananas: buy them in bulk, like they are going out of style. Most recipes will call for a banana or 2. You can buy pre-sliced frozen bananas in very large quantities.

Cheetah spotted bananas: stock up on fresh bananas too. The cheetah spotted ones are the sweetest. Be sure they are "cheetah spotted" and not completely brown. Peel and slice into ¼ inch thick pieces. Store in a freezer bag or container for future use.

Frozen fruits: every recipe is going to call for some kind of frozen fruit. The possibilities are limitless, so buy any frozen fruit you like. Strawberries, blueberries, raspberries, blackberries, cherries, melons, peaches, pineapples, and mangos are some of the most popular.

Fresh fruits: buy and freeze your favorites. Pineapples, mangos, peaches, kiwi, and grapes are some of the popular fruits that are difficult to find already frozen. Just buy the fruit fresh, slice into ¼ inch thick pieces and freeze in freezer bags or containers until you're ready to use them.

Peanut butter: peanut butter can be pretty awesome in frozen treats. Stock up if that's your thing.

Nutella: everyone's hazelnut favorite.

Cocoa powder: sweetened or unsweetened, cocoa powder is found in the chocolate recipes. A lot goes a long way, plus you can usually find it in an easily sealable container.

Milk: chose your flavor. Many healthy options are available like almond, soy, and coconut milk and come in different flavors. The boxed milk can be found on the sell and not refrigerated. You can store these in your pantry until you are ready to use.

Canned coconut milk: not to be confused with boxed or refrigerated coconut milk. Canned coconut milk separates. The top part is usually a thick layer of what is referred to as "coconut cream", and the bottom part is "coconut milk". All recipes will call for the canned milk to be refrigerated. It is okay to store the can in the fridge before it has been opened.

Greek yogurt: Greek yogurt has a thicker consistency than regular yogurt. This helps for a thicker dessert. Its flavor is also a little bit more tart than regular yogurt. Be sure to buy regular, vanilla and low-fat or fat-free varieties.

Toasted nuts: walnuts, pecan, cashews, peanuts. Choose whichever nuts you would like to use. Typically, a garnish.

Coconut flakes: toasted coconut flakes compliment many desserts.

Chocolate chips: used as a garnish and also as chunks run through the machine. Regular size or minis.

Sprinkles: rainbow, colored or chocolate! Jazz up your dessert.

Dark chocolate: choose bars of dark chocolate. Recipes range from 70%-85%.

Cookies: pies and cakes use different cookie crumbs for the crust. Graham crackers, Oreos, and gingersnaps are some of the most popular.

Canola Oil: a few tablespoons of canola oil are added to cookie crumbs to make pie crusts.

Eggs: large.

Pie crusts: frozen pie crusts can cut back on prep time.

Lemons and limes: add a little kick. Many of the refreshing recipes will ask for lemon and lime zest or juice.

Extracts: vanilla, almond, and peppermint are some of the big ones.

Coffee: get your breakfast juice on. Seriously, everyone needs and excuse to eat ice cream for breakfast. So, try some coffee recipes and give yourself a reason.

TASTE HACKING GUIDE

Let's be honest, while smoothies and blended treats can be the easiest to make, things can, and do, go terribly wrong. Not everything turns out the way it should, resulting in an end product being too bitter, too thin, too thick, or even too sweet (yes that is actually a thing). Not to worry, here are some simple fixes for your Yonanas Healthy Dessert Maker®.

1. When it's too bitter

While green veggies can be a main component of smoothies, they can also be the main contributor to that unwelcome bitter taste. But don't remove the greens! Try using baby spinach because it has a gentler flavor. Use sweeter fruits. Try pairing greens with fruits like bananas, pineapples, dates, blueberries, or strawberries. The sweet flavors will complement the bitter greens and make them not as harsh. Stevia, honey, agave nectar, and vanilla are some great natural sweeteners that will help counteract any bitterness, but be careful, a little goes a long way. If a sweet flavor wouldn't be your first choice, opt for some lemon or lime juice. The juice cuts through the bitterness and can create a refreshing, cool taste. Consider adding protein powder too. Not only will it boost protein intake of course, but the powders come in fun flavors that can add a twist to any treat.

2.When it's too sweet

It happens. Every once in a while, you get a super sweet smoothie. The first fix is if you're adding sugar or other sweeteners, just don't. The smallest amount can add an explosion of flavor. Consider using low-glycemic fruits like blackberries, grapefruits or avocados. If using milk or other additives opt for the unsweetened or sugar-free version. And of course, the end-all, be-all, fix-all is to add some lemon or lime juice and get a refreshing burst of flavor instead.

3.When it's too thick

If your smoothies come out too thick, try adding some water, milk, coffee or juice, but be sure not to add too much. Use less frozen and fresher. Sometimes the frozen fruits can be too thick and hard and not produce enough juice to thin out the smoothie. Next time try alternating liquids and solids, putting liquids in first.

4.When it's too thin

Sometimes they come out too thin. We're goin' for smoothies and frozen treats here folks, not juices! If you run into this super common issue, try using fruits with thick skins. Peaches, mangos, dates and apricots make perfect thickeners. Bananas, avocados, and

Greek yogurt are great too. Alternate the adding of liquids and solids. Add fruits and veggies first. This prevents all the liquid from pooling. Guar gum and xanthan gum are great options, especially for alcoholic treats that tend to get runny. Both are gluten-free. They function like gluten and help to bind and create volume. Just like sweeteners, a little of these additives go a long way. Try only using 1/8 of a teaspoon, otherwise, you will have another consistency issue on your hands.

5.When it's too sour

Some desserts are made to be tangy and sour, but then again too much of anything is never a good thing. Try adding more bananas or other sweeter fruits to help off put the sourness. If the recipe calls for milk or other liquids trying to add an additional tablespoon, just don't overdo it or it will get runny. When all else fails, add some sugar or natural sweeteners like honey, agave nectar or stevia.

DOS AND DONTS OF SAFETY WITH YOUR MACHINE

DO use cheetah spotted bananas
DO use frozen fruit
DO have ingredients measured and laid out
DO experiment
DO alternate the adding of ingredients
DO thoroughly clean after every use

DO NOT use ice
DO NOT use fruits with pits
DO NOT submerge base of machine in water
DO NOT use a lot of liquid
DO NOT use gummy candies
DO NOT use hard candies

TROUBLESHOOTING

What is my Yonanas Healthy Dessert Maker® turns off while I'm using it?

Make sure the chute is locked at the 12 o'clock position and has not slipped out. Sometimes if the machine runs for more than 3 minutes, or gets hot, it will shut off. If everything is as it should be, let the machine rest for 5 minutes and try again.

What if can't get my machine to turn on?

Make sure the unit is plugged in and the chute is locked at 12 o'clock position. You should hear and feel the chute click into place when assembling the machine.

What is it smells like it's burning?

There could be residue on the motor.

What if nothing comes out after I put fruit in?

Make sure you are using enough fruit to push everything through the machine.

Ice Creams Using Bananas

Creamy Caramelized Banana and Pecan Ice Cream

A delicious recipe with only 4 ingredients. You can't go wrong with caramelized bananas and toasted pecans. And it's Paleo approved!

Serves: 4
Total Time: 8 hours 15 minutes

INGREDIENTS:

4 bananas, sliced and frozen
3 Tbsp. ghee (clarified butter)
½ cup coconut milk, canned and chilled
1/2 cup toasted pecans, chopped

PREPARATION:

1. Slice 2 bananas and store overnight, or for at least 6 hours, in a freezer bag or container
2. Slice remaining 2 bananas into ½ in. thick rounds.
3. Melt the ghee in a shallow pan over med/high heat until it foams and turns slightly brown.
4. Add banana slices to the ghee and continue cooking until the bottoms turn brown.
5. Flip, and brown opposite sides as well.
6. Take caramelized bananas and scrape everything, including the brown pieces, into a freezer bag or container.
7. Freeze overnight for at least 6 hours.
8. Remove caramelized bananas from freezer and let sit on the counter for about 5 minutes.
9. Empty both batches of frozen bananas into your Yonanas Healthy Dessert Maker®.
10. Toss a few bananas and a little bit of the coconut milk into the machine.
11. Push down on the plunger and repeat this step, alternating bananas and coconut milk until everything is used.
13. Gently mix the pecans into the ice cream with a spoon.

Breakfast of Champions Coffee Ice Cream

Every morning requires coffee. Okay, sometimes every afternoon...and every evening too. The point is that this coffee ice cream can be enjoyed at any time during the day or night, but why not use it as a great excuse to have ice cream for breakfast? Breakfast of champions. And it's dairy free!

Serves: 2
Total Time: 10 minutes

INGREDIENTS:

4 bananas, sliced and frozen
¼ cup espresso or coffee, room temperature
½ tsp vanilla extract
sugar to taste

PREPARATION:

1. Brew the espresso or coffee.
2. Add sugar to desired taste.
3. Let cool to room temperature.
4. Once at room temperature mix in the vanilla extract.
5. Alternate adding bananas and coffee into the Yonanas Healthy Dessert Maker®
6. Press down with the plunger.
7. Repeat steps 5 and 6 until all ingredients are used
8. Enjoy immediately or freeze for later awesomeness.

Chocolate and Peanut Butter Swirl Ice Cream

Chocolate and Peanut Butter were created for each other. Both are great independently but are enjoyed better together. Get your fix with this 3-ingredient ice cream.

Serves: 1-2 depending on how much you want to share
Total Time: 5 minutes

INGREDIENTS:

2 bananas, sliced and frozen
2 Tbsp. peanut butter
1 Tbsp. sweetened cocoa powder

PREPARATION:

1. Toss half the frozen bananas into the chute.
2. Add 1 Tbsp. of the peanut butter and ½ a Tbsp. of the cocoa powder.
3. Turn on the machine and push down the plunger.
4. Repeat steps 1 and 2.
5. Enjoy. Share if you must.

Quadruple Threat Chocolate Ice Cream

There is no such thing as too much chocolate, and this recipe proves that. 5 ingredients, 4 of which are chocolate. Take 5 minutes and feed your need.

Serves: 4
Total Time: 5 minutes

INGREDIENTS:

2 bananas, sliced and frozen
1 cup chocolate almond milk
½ cup sweetened cocoa powder
½ cup chocolate chips
½ cup chocolate sprinkles for topping

PREPARATION:

1. Add a few bananas, a splash of the almond milk, a dash of cocoa powder and some chocolate chips to the Yonanas Healthy Dessert Maker®
2. Turn the machine to "on" and press down with the plunger.
3. Repeat steps 1 and 2 until all ingredients are used.
4. Top with sprinkles.
5. Indulge.

Strawberries and Cream Banana Ice Cream

Moms are always dressing up fruit to make it more enticing, and strawberries and cream are classic. This recipe will bring you back to childhood bliss.

Serves: 2
Total Time: 5 minutes

INGREDIENTS:

2 bananas, sliced and frozen
2 Tbsp. heavy cream
½ cup strawberries, frozen
½ tsp vanilla

PREPARATION:

1. Combine heavy cream and vanilla.
2. Insert half of the bananas, half of the strawberries and half of the cream mixture into the Yonanas Health Dessert Maker®.
3. Turn on the machine and press down with the plunger.
4. Add the remaining ingredients and plunge again.
5. Tada! Strawberries and cream banana ice cream!
Enjoy as soft serve of freeze for 3 hours for scoopable ice cream

Easy Peasy Chocolate Peanut Butter Soft Serve

It's called Easy Peasy Chocolate Peanut Butter Banana Soft Serve for a reason. This is a super easy, healthy, delicious recipe that a 5-year-old could make. Well, a 5-year-old could give instructions because a 5-year-old should probably not be using a Yonanas Healthy Dessert maker®. Anyhow, take a few minutes and see how easy it is for yourself.

Serves: 3
Total Time: 5 minutes

INGREDIENTS:

3 bananas, sliced and frozen
3 Tbsp. peanut butter
2 Tbsp. sweetened cocoa powder

PREPARATION:

1. Mix the cocoa powder and peanut butter by hand.
2. Add one banana and ¼ of the peanut butter mixture to your Yonanas Healthy Dessert Maker®.
3. Press down with the plunger.
4. Repeat steps 2 and 3 twice more. You should end up with ¼ of the peanut butter mixture left over.
5. Hand mix the remaining peanut butter mixture with the soft serve and an added texture.
6. Enjoy immediately.

Refreshing Orange Soft Serve

Okay, be healthy. But make it fun! Try this sugar-free, dairy free, gluten free, paleo approved recipe. The super easy 2 ingredient recipe is ultra-refreshing and 100% all natural. Eat as much as your heart desires.

Serves: 2
Total Time:5 minutes

INGREDIENTS:

2 bananas, sliced and frozen
1 cup orange pieces, frozen

PREPARATION:

1. Add ½ the banana slices and all the oranges to the Yonanas Healthy Dessert Maker®.
2. Plunge.
3. Add the remaining bananas and plunge.
4. Enjoy.

Rockin' Raspberry Dark Chocolate Chunk Ice Cream

Imagine a satiny piece of dark chocolate with a rich raspberry filling. The flavors meld together in your mouth creating a taste that lingers not quite long enough. Now imagine that taste as cool and refreshing and with half the calories. Yes, it exists, and in less than 10 minutes you can experience it.

Serves: 2
Total Time: 10 minutes

INGREDIENTS:

2 bananas, sliced and frozen
2 oz. 70% dark chocolate
1 cup raspberries, frozen

PREPARATION:

1. Chop up the dark chocolate into tiny pieces and set aside.
2. Take half the bananas, ½ cup of raspberries and about half of the chocolate.
3. Plunge.
4.. Repeat steps 1 and 2.
5. Enjoy.

Tutti-Frutti

Tutti-frutti means "all fruits" in Italian. You're welcome for that awesome bit of trivia. You'll thank me more once you've tried this recipe. While it doesn't have ALL the fruits we love, it does check quite a few of those boxes with mangos, strawberries, and bananas.

Serves: 4
Total Time: 5 minutes

INGREDIENTS:

2 bananas, sliced and frozen
2 cups mangos, frozen
1 cup strawberries, frozen

PREPARATION:

1. Alternate adding fruits into the Yonanas Healthy Dessert Maker®.
2. That's it!

Tropical Dream Ice Cream

This recipe will make you think you're on a tropical vacation, lying on a beach being served fruity treats with paper umbrellas. We can't always be in paradise, but we sure can pretend with this tasty treat.

Serves: 3-4
Total Time: 10 minutes

INGREDIENTS:

3 bananas, sliced and frozen
 1 Tbsp. coconut milk, canned and chilled
½ cup pineapple chunks, frozen
½ cup mango chunks, frozen
½ tsp vanilla extract
¼ cup toasted coconut, shredded
¼ cup salted cashews of macadamia nuts, chopped

PREPARATION:

1. Mix the vanilla extract and coconut milk and set aside.
2. Put a portion of the bananas, pineapples and mangos into the Yonanas Healthy Dessert Maker®.
3. Press down with the plunger.
4. Repeat step 2 and then add the coconut and vanilla mixture.
5. Press down with the plunger.
6. Repeat step 2 again, using the last of the bananas, pineapples, and mangos.
7. Garnish with nuts and coconut. Go ahead, add a little paper umbrella, you know you want to.
8. Enjoy your tropical treat.

Mean Green Avocado Ice Cream

Avocados are a versatile fruit. They are used in all kinds of desserts these days to create a healthier option, and ice cream is no different. Brace yourself for all sorts of awesome with this avocado ice cream recipe.

Serves: 2
Total Time: 5 minutes

INGREDIENTS:

2 bananas, sliced and frozen
1 avocado, cubed and frozen
1 cup frozen mango chunks
½ cup nuts of your choice

PREPARATION:

1. Put half the banana slices in the Yonanas Healthy Dessert Maker®.
2. Press down with the plunger.
3. Add the avocado and mango chunks and plunge again.
4. Top with nuts.
5. Enjoy.

Better Than Basic Pumpkin Spice Ice Cream

Pumpkin spice treats. You either love 'em or you hate 'em. Even if you're one of those that rolls their eyes when pumpkin spice season comes around, give this ice cream treat a try, just to say you did. Your secret's safe with us.

Serves: 6
Total Time: 5 minutes (+freezing time)

INGREDIENTS:

4 bananas, sliced and frozen
1 ½ tsp pumpkin spice
1 cup canned pumpkin, frozen into cubes
½ cup maple syrup

PREPARATION:

1. Freeze the canned pumpkin into cubes using an ice cube tray.
2. Alternately feed bananas and cubed pumpkin into the Yonanas Healthy Dessert Maker®.
3. Add in ¼ cup of maple syrup.
4. Plunge.
5. Repeat steps 2, 3 and 4.
6. Hand mix the pumpkin spice in with the soft serve ice cream.
7. Enjoy guiltlessly.

Banana Blueberry Blast

Try this frozen favorite in just 5 minutes. It's super easy, super-fast, super inexpensive, and super flavorful. The tart blueberries, sweet banana, and vanilla make for the perfect frozen treat.

Serves: 2
Total Time: 5 minutes

INGREDIENTS:

2 bananas, sliced and frozen
1 tsp vanilla extract
¼ cup frozen blueberries

PREPARATION:

1. Insert half of the bananas and half of the blueberries into the Yonanas Healthy Dessert Maker®.
2. Press down on the plunger.
3. Add the remaining fruit and vanilla.
4. Plunge.
5. Enjoy

Not Yo Mama's Ants On a Log Ice Cream

See what we did there? Yo Mama's...Yonanas.... Well Yonanas Healthy Dessert Maker® can now transform that delectable little banana treat your mom used to make for you. The banana is no longer a log but creamy soft serve ice cream.

Serves: 2
Total Time: 5 minutes

INGREDIENTS:

4 bananas, sliced and frozen
3 Tbsp. creamy peanut butter
½ cup chocolate covered raisins

PREPARATION:

1. Add ¼ of the bananas and 1 Tbsp. of peanut butter into the chute.
2. Press down on the plunger.
3. Repeat steps 1 and 2 until all ingredients are used.
4. Top with chocolate covered raisins.
5. Enjoy as if you were a kid again.

Nutella®, Need We Say More, Ice Cream

Nutella® is the newest craze, and for good reason. If you don't know, Nutella® is a hazelnut cocoa spread that you can put on just about anything. This recipe takes the creamy goodness to a whole 'notha level but turning it into ice cream. Prepare for a life changer.

Serves: 2
Total Time: 5 minutes

INGREDIENTS:

4 bananas, sliced and frozen
½ cup Nutella®

PREPARATION:

1. Fill the chute with bananas and some Nutella®.
2. Plunge.
3. Repeat steps 1 and 2 until all ingredients are used.
4. Enjoy, enjoy, enjoy. Share if you must.

Angel's Apricot Ice Cream

Dried fruit can have a super sweet flavor and a chewy texture. Dried apricots compliment the creamy frozen bananas. Get a deliciously chewy and creamy texture with this recipe.

Serves: 1
Total Time: 5 minutes

INGREDIENTS:

2 bananas, sliced and frozen
¾ cup dried apricots

PREPARATION:

1. Insert half the bananas and half the apricots.
2. Plunge.
3. Add remaining apricots first followed by the remaining bananas.
4. Plunge.
5. Enjoy.

Crunchy Almond Peach Ice Cream

Every now and again ice cream deserves a crunch. This recipe throws in a few roasted almonds for an extra crunch with your cream.

Serves: 2
Total Time: 5 minutes

INGREDIENTS:

2 bananas, sliced and frozen
5 peach slices, frozen
½ cup roasted almonds, chopped

PREPARATION:

1. Alternate adding bananas, peaches, and nuts into the Yonanas Healthy Dessert Maker ®.
2. Press down on the plunger.
3. Repeat steps 1 and 2 until all ingredients are used.
4. Enjoy

Granny's Apple Pie Ice Cream

Granny's apple pie was always a special treat. It meant holidays. Thanksgiving, Christmas, 4th of July, Memorial Day…And it always cooled on a ledge near the kitchen. While this recipe probably won't top her homemade apple pie, it sure will be a close second.

Serves: 4
Total Time: 5 minutes

INGREDIENTS:

5 dried apple slices
2 frozen bananas
2 Tbsp. applesauce
¼ tsp cinnamon

PREPARATION:

1. Mix the cinnamon and applesauce in a bowl and set aside.
2. Add half the banana slices, 3 apple slices and half the applesauce mixture to the Yonanas Healthy Dessert Maker®.
3. Press down with the plunger.
4. Repeat steps 2 and 3.
5. Indulge.

Goodness Gracious Green Tea Ice Cream

Another great breakfast ice cream! Get your dose of green tea pick me up early in the morning. Of course, this recipe can be enjoyed anytime, but we love an excuse to have ice cream for breakfast.

Serves: 2
Total Time: 5 minutes

INGREDIENTS:

3 bananas, sliced and frozen
2 tsp matcha powder
1 Tbsp. sweetened condensed milk

PREPARATION:

1. Alternate adding ingredients into Yonanas Healthy Dessert Maker® in thirds.
2. Plunge after every third.
3. Repeat until all ingredients are used.
4. Enjoy.

Chocolate Covered Cherry Ice Cream

Chocolate covered cherries aren't just bite sized treats anymore. That same flavor can be had in a creamy, smooth, soft-serve ice cream in minutes using your dessert maker.

Serves: 2
Total Time: 10 minutes

INGREDIENTS:

2 bananas, sliced and frozen

I cup frozen cherries, pitted

½ tsp coconut oil

¼ cup chocolate chips

PREPARATION:

1. Add half the bananas and ½ cup of cherries to the Yonanas Healthy Dessert Maker®.
2. Press down on the plunger.
3. Repeat steps 1 and 2.
4. Combine coconut oil and chocolate chips. Microwave for 1-2 minutes until melted. Be careful not to burn the chocolate.
5. Pour melted chocolate over the cherry ice cream.
6. Enjoy.

Very Berry Frozen Yogurt

Taste the tang with this sweet and sour recipe. If a blueberry tart could be frozen yogurt, this would be it. Enjoy the silky, smooth texture and creaminess without sacrificing the sharp, sour flavor.

Serves: 6
Total Time: 10 minutes

INGREDIENTS:

4 cups frozen blueberries
1 banana, sliced and frozen
1 cup plain Greek yogurt

1 tbsp. blackcurrant syrup
½ cup sugar
¼ cup frozen orange juice concentrate

PREPARATION:

1. Combine yogurt, syrup, and sugar. Set aside.
2. Combine blueberries and banana slices. Set aside.
3. Add some of the fruit mixture and some of the yogurt mixture to the Yonanas Healthy Dessert Maker®.
4. Press down with the plunger.
5. Add more of both of the mixture and some orange juice concentrate. Top with more fruit.
6. Plunge.
7. Continue until all ingredients are used.
8. Mix well to fully combine ingredients.

Chocolate Candy Cane Ice Cream

Is it Christmas yet? Even if it's in the dead of summer you can still pretend it's the most wonderful time of the year with this pepper minty fresh ice cream.

Serves: 2
Total Time: 5 minutes

INGREDIENTS:

4 Tbsp. sweetened cocoa powder
2 bananas, frozen and sliced

1 candy cane (or peppermint candy), crushed
¼ chocolate chips

PREPARATION:

1. Combine ingredients.
2. Add mixture to your Yonanas Healthy Dessert Maker®.
3. Press down with the plunger when the chute gets full.
4. Enjoy!

Chunky Monkey Cinnamon Ice Cream

Chunky, chewy, cinnamon perfection. Trick yourself into thinking you're splurging with this cinnamon-bun tasting vegan ice cream. No guilty feelings here.

Serves: 2
Total Time: 7 minutes

INGREDIENTS:

4 bananas, sliced and frozen
4 dates, chopped
2 Tbsp. almond milk
1 tsp sugar

½ tsp vanilla extract
½ tsp cinnamon
¼ cup walnuts, chopped

PREPARATION:

1. Mix almond milk, sugar, vanilla extract, and cinnamon. Set aside.
2. Combine bananas and dates.
3. Alternate adding fruits and sugar mixtures to your Yonanas Healthy Dessert Maker®.
4. Press down with the plunger when the chute gets full.
5. Stir in walnuts.
6. Enjoy!

PBJ Like Mom Made

Just about everyone's Mom made peanut butter and jelly sandwiches. It's a childhood lunch staple. We have turned that staple into an ice cream. No crust cutting needed here, just good 'ole PB&J.

Serves: 2
Total Time: 5 minutes

INGREDIENTS:

2 bananas, frozen and sliced
1 cup mixed berries, frozen
1 Tbsp. peanut butter

PREPARATION:

1. Alternate adding ingredients to your Yonanas Healthy Dessert Maker®.
2. Press down with the plunger when the chute gets full.
3. Enjoy!

Chocolate Chip Cookie Dough Ice Cream

You read that correctly! You can have homemade chocolate chip cookie dough ice cream in just minutes. We promise you'll like this healthy alternative as much as the store-bought brands.

Serves: 2
Total Time: 2 minutes

INGREDIENTS:

2 bananas, sliced and frozen
3 heaping spoonfuls of vegan cookie dough

PREPARATION:

1. Alternate adding ingredients to your Yonanas Healthy Dessert Maker®.
2. Press down with the plunger when the chute gets full.
3. Enjoy!

Hot Chocolate Ice Cream

So we know it's an oxymoron, but sometimes it's too hot outside for hot chocolate. You must answer that craving, and now it's possible in the coolest of ways.

Serves: 2
Total Time: 5 minutes

INGREDIENTS:

2 bananas, sliced and frozen
2 Tbsp. mini marshmallows
1 packet of your favorite hot chocolate mix
1 Tbsp. chocolate sauce

PREPARATION:

1. Sprinkle the hot chocolate mix on the bananas.
2. Add the bananas to your Yonanas Healthy Dessert Maker®.
3. Press down with the plunger when the chute gets full.
4. Top with marshmallows and chocolate sauce.
5. Enjoy!

Perfect Pumpkin Pie Ice Cream

Something about vanilla, cinnamon, and nutmeg makes us happy. Ahh, that's it... Pumpkin pie. So why not a Yonanas pumpkin pie? We couldn't think of s reason why not either.

Serves: 5
Total Time: 10 minutes + 3 hours freeze time

INGREDIENTS:

10 bananas, sliced and frozen
2 cups gingersnaps, crumbled
1 can pumpkin puree
1 tsp vanilla extract
1 tsp cinnamon
½ tsp nutmeg

PREPARATION:

1. Mix pumpkin puree, vanilla, cinnamon, and nutmeg in a bowl.
2. Spoon mixture into ice cube trays and freeze for 3 hours.
3. Insert 3 cubes and 2 bananas at a time into your Yonanas Healthy Dessert Maker®.
4. Press down with the plunger.
5. Repeat steps 3 and 4 five times until all ingredients are used.
6. Enjoy!

Banana-Free Ice Cream

Peach Perfect Frozen Yogurt

Add a little sweetness to your life with this 4-ingredient recipe. Enjoy the sweet peaches with a touch of tang. So, creamy you wouldn't believe it's made with frozen fruit.

Serves: 4
Total Time: 10 minutes

INGREDIENTS:

3 ½ cups frozen peaches, chopped
1 Tbsp. lemon juice
½ cup nonfat plain yogurt
½ cup of sugar

PREPARATION:

1. Mix lemon juice and yogurt together. Set aside.
2. Run some peaches through the Yonanas Healthy Dessert Maker chute and press down on the plunger.
3. Add more peaches, half the yogurt mixture and half the sugar.
4. Press down on the plunger.
5. Repeat steps 3 and 4.
6. Add the remaining peaches and press the plunger.
7. Stir to completely combine flavors.
8. Enjoy.

Bomb Berry Frozen Yogurt

Tantalizingly tart. This blackberry recipe is an excellent way to kick-start summer. Totally refreshing.

Serves: 6
Total Time: 10 minutes

INGREDIENTS:

6 Tbsp. sugar
3 cups frozen blackberries
1Tbsp lemon juice
¾ cup low-fat plain yogurt

PREPARATION:

1. Combine sugar, lemon juice and yogurt in a small bowl. Set aside.
2. Alternate adding and plunging blackberries and yogurt mixture into your Yonanas Healthy Dessert Maker® until all ingredients are used.
3. Enjoy.

Wacky Watermelon Frozen Yogurt

The quintessential summer fruit is watermelon. Impress all your friends with this unique treat. No seeds, no juice, no mess.

Serves: 8
Total Time: 20 minutes

INGREDIENTS:

4 cups seedless watermelon, diced and frozen
1 cup low-fat vanilla yogurt
1 Tbsp. lime juice
¼ cup water
¼ cup sugar

PREPARATION:

1. Heat water and sugar in a small pot over med/high heat until sugar is completely dissolved. Set aside to cool to room temperature (it will turn into syrup).
2. Combine the syrup mixture, lime juice, and yogurt.
3. Alternate adding watermelon pieces and spoonfuls of syrup to your Yonanas Healthy Dessert Maker until all ingredients are used. Be sure to press down on the plunger when full.
4. Enjoy.

No Churn Almond Peach Ice Cream

Fluffy and creamy, whipped almond peach ice cream! Yum. The marshmallow fluff and milk give this ice cream a unique texture. It takes creamy to a whole 'nother level.

Serves: 6
Total Time: 3 hours 20 minutes

INGREDIENTS:

3 cups frozen peaches, sliced
2 Tbsp. lemon juice
1 ½ cups marshmallow fluff
1 cup low-fat milk
½ tsp almond extract

PREPARATION:

1. Mix lemon juice, milk and almond extract. Set aside.
2. Freeze milk mixture for about 3 hours in ice cube trays. You want this milk to become slushy.
3. Toss in 1 cup of peaches, a couple spoonfuls of marshmallow fluff and a few cubes of the milk mixture into the Yonanas Healthy Dessert Maker® chute.
4. Press down on the plunger.
5. Repeat steps 3 and 4 until all ingredients are used.
6. Enjoy.

Heavenly Melon Fro-Yo

Melons have a way of reminding us of spring and summer. The weather is no longer cold, and we are in search of something cool and refreshing. This recipe delivers on all counts.

Serves: 4
Total Time: 10 minutes

INGREDIENTS:

3 cups frozen melons
1 Tbsp. lemon juice
½ cup nonfat plain yogurt
½ cup sugar

PREPARATION:

1. Combine lemon juice, yogurt, and sugar. Set aside.
2. Add ½ the melon and ½ the yogurt to the Yonanas Healthy Dessert Maker ®.
3. Press down with the plunger.
4. Repeat steps 2 and 3.
5. Enjoy.

Raspberry Lemonade Frozen Yogurt

We found your midafternoon treat! How refreshing is lemonade by itself? The sweet and sour flavor gives that little-needed zing. But add raspberries and turn it into frozen yogurt, and you have the perfect afternoon refresher. Don't drink your lemonade, eat it with a spoon.

Serves: 4
Total Time: 10 minutes

INGREDIENTS:

3 cups vanilla nonfat yogurt
2 tsp lemon zest
1 cup frozen raspberries
¼ cup sugar
¼ cup lemon juice

PREPARATION:

1. Combine yogurt, lemon zest, sugar and lemon juice. Set aside.
2. Add ½ the raspberries and ½ the yogurt mixture to your Yonanas Healthy Dessert Maker®.
3. Press down with the plunger.
4. Repeat steps 2 and 3.
5. If consistency is too runny freeze for a few hours, or enjoy immediately.

All-star Raspberry Coconut Ice Cream

Coconutty cool and creamy. The smooth, rich texture will fool you into thinking this recipe is loaded full of sugar. Not to worry, it's a calorie friendly treat.

Serves: 4
Total Time: 5 minutes

INGREDIENTS:

4 tsp maple syrup
1 ½ cups frozen raspberries
1 cup full fat coconut cream from canned and chilled coconut milk
¼ cup coconut milk, canned and chilled

PREPARATION:

1. Combine coconut cream, coconut milk, and maple syrup.
2. Add ½ the raspberries and half the coconut mixture to the Yonanas Healthy Dessert Maker ®.
3. Press down with the plunger.
4. Repeat steps 2 and 3.
5. Indulge.

Intense Chocolate Chip and Raspberry Coconut Ice Cream

Tarty and sweet, chock-full of raspberries and chocolate. This recipe has a hint of vanilla that sets it above the rest.

Serves: 4
Total Time: 8 hours 10 minutes

INGREDIENTS:

4 tsp vanilla extract
3 cups coconut milk
I cup frozen raspberries
¾ cup chocolate chips
½ cup honey

PREPARATION:

1. Mix coconut milk and vanilla. Freeze in ice cube trays for 8 hours or overnight.
2. Add a few cubes of the milk mixture, half the raspberries, half the chocolate, and half the honey.
3. Press down with the plunger.
4. Repeat steps 2 and 3.
5. Enjoy.

Minute Melon Sherbet

Sherbet was always a fun treat as a kid. We thought we were winning by getting a super special, sugary treat, and Mom though she was winning by giving us a healthier version of ice cream. Everyone wins with Sherbet. And this recipe is no different. Less sugar but without sacrificing the flavor.

Serves: 2
Total Time: 3 minutes

INGREDIENTS:

3 cups of assorted melons, frozen

PREPARATION:

1. Toss in your melons.
2. Push down on the plunger.
3. Repeat steps until all the melon is gone.
4. Be amazed at how easy this was and enjoy your instant treat.

Sorbet

Ridiculously Simply Raspberry Spinach Sorbet

It's so easy! With only 2 ingredients there is ZERO reason to not try this recipe.

Serves: 1
Total Time: 10 minutes

INGREDIENTS:

16 frozen raspberries
¼ cup frozen spinach

PREPARATION:

1. Combine raspberries and frozen spinach.
2. Insert into Yonanas Healthy Dessert Maker®.
3. Press down on the plunger.
4. Enjoy!

Miller's Mango Sorbet

Icy. Cool. Refreshing. Healthy. No sugar added here. All real fruit. All really good.

Serves: 2
Total Time: 10 minutes

INGREDIENTS:

2 bananas, sliced and frozen
1 cup frozen mango
1 cup frozen pineapple

PREPARATION:

1. Run half the bananas through your Yonanas Healthy Dessert Maker®.
2. Press down on the plunger.
3. Repeat steps 1 and 2 with mango, pineapple, and remaining bananas.
4. Stir to mix the flavors.
5. Enjoy.

Exotic Papaya-Lime Sorbet

Imagine sitting under a palapa on a white sand beach with turquoise blue water, sipping a fruity concoction. That fruity blend is likely something very similar to this Exotic Papaya-Lime Sorbet. Try this recipe and transport your sense to paradise.

Serves: 8
Total Time: 30 minutes

INGREDIENTS:

8 cups frozen papaya
2 Tbsp. lime juice
2 pinches of salt
1 tsp lime zest
½ cup water
½ cup sugar
¼ cup coconut milk, canned and chilled

PREPARATION:

1. Boil water and sugar over med/high heat until the sugar is completely dissolved (about 3-5 minutes). Be sure to stir constantly, so it doesn't burn. Set aside to cool.
2. Add ¼ of the papayas, ¼ of the syrup, 1 tablespoon of the milk, ½ tablespoon lime juice, ¼ teaspoon of the zest, and a small pinch of salt to your Yonanas Healthy Dessert Maker ®
3. Press down on the plunger.
4. Repeat steps 2 and 3 about 4 more times until all the ingredients are used.
5. Enjoy.

Fresh and Fruity Pineapple-Coconut Sorbet

Bring summer to your kitchen. All the fun ingredients are used to create a fruit cocktail sorbet you can't get enough of. Mix sweet and sour and add a dash of zesty flavor with the crushed ginger. Perfection.

Serves: 8
Total Time: 25 minutes

INGREDIENTS:

3 ¼ in. thick ginger, peeled and crushed
2 tsp lime juice
1 pineapple, chopped and frozen
½ cup sugar
½ cup coconut milk, canned and chilled

PREPARATION:

1. Simmer coconut milk, sugar and ginger over medium heat. Bring to a boil. Set aside.
2. Once the mixture has cooled strain into a bowl and set aside.
3. Run ½ the pineapple mixture, ½ the coconut mixture and ½ the lime juice through your Yonanas Healthy Dessert Maker®.
4. Press down on the plunger.
5. Repeat steps 3 and 4.
6. Enjoy.

Show-stopping Chocolate Earl Grey Sorbet

While this may not be one of the easy peasy, 2 ingredient recipes, it is worth the time and effort. The tangy citrus marries the chocolate creating an indescribable flavor.

Serves: 6
Total Time: 2 hours 45 minutes

INGREDIENTS:

4 Earl Grey tea bags
4 cups water
1 cup unsweetened cocoa powder
1 oz. bitter chocolate, chopped
¾ cup sugar

PREPARATION:

1. Boil water and sugar.
2. Add tea bags to water/sugar mixture and remove from heat. Step for 15 minutes.
3. Toss out the tea bags and return the mixture to med/high heat.
4. Add cocoa powder and whisk until smooth.
5. Reduce heat and simmer for 20 minutes.
6. Remove from heat, adding chocolate until it is completely melted.
7. Strain the mixture and freeze for 2 hours.
8. Break into chunks and feed into your Yonanas Healthy Dessert Maker®, pressing down on the plunger when the chute is full.

Florescent Tropical Sorbet

This recipe is bright and colorful and will catch anyone's eye. But looks aren't the only appeal. It is made with real fruit and sugar-free.

Serves: 4
Total Time: 5 minutes

INGREDIENTS:

1 ½ cups frozen mango, chopped
¾ cup frozen strawberries
¾ cup frozen pineapple chunks

PREPARATION:

1. Add fruit in alternating order to the Yonanas Healthy Dessert Maker® until all the fruit is used.
2. Press down with the plunger when the chute gets full.
3. Enjoy.

Cranberry Crush Sorbet

All you need to make great sorbet is a couple of ingredients. Literally. Just 2. Mingle the sour flavor of cranberries with the sweet taste of pineapple, and you're set.

Serves: 3
Total Time: 15 minutes + 2 hours freeze time

INGREDIENTS:

2 ½ cups frozen pineapple chunks
1 ½ cups cranberry juice

PREPARATION:

1. Freeze cranberry juice in a bowl for 2 hours, or until slushy.
2. Alternate adding spoonfuls of the cranberry slush and pineapple chunks to your Yonanas Healthy Dessert Maker®.
3. Press down with the plunger when the chute gets full.
4. Repeat until all ingredients are used.
5. Enjoy.

Life Changing Lemon Raspberry Sorbet

Is it life changing because it's so simple, using only 2 ingredients, or because it tastes oh so good? We think both, but you decide.

Serves: 1
Total Time: 5 minutes

INGREDIENTS:

16 frozen raspberries
1 tsp lemon zest

PREPARATION:

1. Insert raspberries and lemon zest to the Yonanas Healthy Dessert Maker®.
2. Press down with the plunger.
3. Enjoy.

Sweet and Sour Watermelon Sorbet

It's not called Sweet and Sour Watermelon Sorbet for nothin'. This recipe is just that. Sweet watermelon with sour lemon juice. Zesty. Sweet. Refreshing.

Serves: 4
Total Time: 15 minutes

INGREDIENTS:

1 Tbsp. lemon juice
½ seedless watermelon, frozen and chopped

PREPARATION:

1. Feed the frozen watermelon chunks and lemon juice into the Yonanas Healthy Dessert Maker®.
2. Press down with the plunger.
3. Enjoy.

Not Your Average Mango Sorbet

Average this recipe is not. It's not just mangos, but sweet simple syrup and a hint of lime juice for a refreshing kick.

Serves: 8
Total Time: 10 minutes

INGREDIENTS:

4 mangos, chopped and frozen
2 Tbsp. lime juice
1 cup simple syrup

PREPARATION:

1. Feed 1 cup of frozen mangos into the Yonanas Healthy Dessert Maker® chute.
2. Top with ¼ of the simple syrup and ½ a tablespoon of lime juice.
3. Press down with the plunger.
4. Repeat 4 times until all ingredients are used.
5. Enjoy.

Clearly Cantaloupe

We love this recipe because...well...cantaloupe. Take this sweet summer treat and turn it into this unique frozen treat!

Serves: 6
Total Time: 10 minutes

INGREDIENTS:

4 cups frozen cantaloupe chunks
2 Tbsp. lemon juice
1 cup sugar
½ cup water

PREPARATION:

1. Boil water and sugar on med/high heat, stirring constantly until fully dissolved. Set aside and refrigerate.
2. Add 1 cup of cantaloupe chunks, ½ tablespoon of lemon juice and ¼ of the syrup mixture into the Yonanas Healthy Dessert Maker ®.
3. Press down on the plunger.
4. Repeat steps 2 and 3 until all ingredients are used.
5. Enjoy

Gilbert's Grape Sorbet

Frozen grapes are the healthiest of snacks, tricking your senses into thinking you're eating frozen candies. It has always been my family's movie night snack of choice, so what could be better than green grape sorbet? You'll think you're eating a sugary treat.

Serves: 2
Total Time: 2 minutes

INGREDIENTS:

3 cups frozen green grapes

PREPARATION:

1. Toss grapes into your Yonanas Healthy Frozen Dessert Maker®.
2. Press down with the plunger when the chute gets full.
3. You're done! Enjoy.

Instant Pineapple Sorbet

Sweet pineapples and a touch of lemon juice with have your taste buds asking for more of this sorbet. Not to worry, you don't have to share if you don't want to.

Serves: 1-2
Total Time: 2 minutes

INGREDIENTS:

3 Tbsp. simple syrup
1 cup frozen pineapple chunks
1 tsp lemon juice

PREPARATION:

1. Place all ingredients into the Yonanas Healthy Dessert Maker®.
2. Press down with the plunger.
3. Enjoy!

Perfect Peach Sorbet

Treat yourself to some syrupy flavored sorbet. Chunks of peaches laced with orange juice and maple syrup make for a sweet and tangy treat.

Serves: 1-2
Total Time: 2 minutes

INGREDIENTS:

3 Tbsp. maple syrup
1 cup peaches, sliced and frozen
1 tsp orange juice

PREPARATION:

1. Place all ingredients into the Yonanas Healthy Dessert Maker®.
2. Press down with the plunger.
3. Enjoy!

Rawesome Honeydew Melon Sorbet

Honeydew is underrated. Cantaloupe and watermelons are always stealing the show, but not with this frozen treat! Get in on this sweet and refreshing action.

Serves: 1-2
Total Time: 2 minutes

INGREDIENTS:

3 Tbsp. simple syrup
1 cup frozen honeydew melon chunks
1 tsp orange juice

PREPARATION:

1. Place all ingredients into the Yonanas Healthy Dessert Maker®.
2. Press down with the plunger.
3. Enjoy!

Cool Creamy Raspberry Sorbet

Simple and smooth. Raspberry sorbet. Easy to make and instantly enjoy.

Serves: 1-2
Total Time: 2 minutes

INGREDIENTS:

3 Tbsp. simple syrup
1 cup frozen raspberries
1 tsp lemon juice

PREPARATION:

1. Place all ingredients into the Yonanas Healthy Dessert Maker®.
2. Press down with the plunger.
3. Enjoy!

Sweet and Creamy Pineapple Mango Sorbet

Change up your pineapple sorbet experience by adding some lime juice and mangos. It will be a Caribbean summer in your kitchen.

Serves: 5
Total Time:15 minutes

INGREDIENTS:

2 cups frozen pineapple chunks
2 cups frozen mango chunks
2 Tbsp. lime juice
1 cup sugar

PREPARATION:

1. Add ½ cup of the pineapple, ½ cup of the mangos, ½ Tbsp of lime juice, and ¼ cup of the sugar to your Yonanas Healthy Dessert Maker®.
2. Press down on the plunger.
3. Repeat steps 1 and 2 until all ingredients are used.
4. Enjoy.

Silky Smooth Strawberry and Raspberry Sorbet Pops

Refresh yourself and your mouth with this berry sorbet. Let it melt in your mouth and rejuvenate your senses.

Serves: 2
Total Time: 10 minutes + 3 hours freeze time

INGREDIENTS:

1 ½ cups coconut milk, canned and chilled
1 Tbsp. Lemon juice
1 tsp honey
½ cup frozen strawberries
½ cup frozen raspberries

PREPARATION:

1.Mix the coconut milk, lemon juice, and honey. Set aside.
2. Alternate adding strawberries, raspberries and milk mixture to the Yonanas Healthy Dessert Maker®.
3. Press down with the plunger.
4. Spoon sorbet into 2 popsicle trays and freeze for 3 hours.

Tasty Tart Peach Lime Sorbet

This multi-ingredient recipe has a satisfyingly crisp flavor. Sugary meets zesty, and we love it.

Serves: 8
Total Time: 4 hours 30 minutes

INGREDIENTS:

6 Tbsp. lime juice
2 cups frozen peaches, sliced
2 Tbsp. light corn syrup
1 ½ cups water
1 tsp lime zest
½ cup sugar
¼ tsp salt

PREPARATION:

1. Heat water, sugar and corn syrup over med/high heat until the sugar is completely dissolved.
2. Add peaches to the syrup mixture and reduce heat.
3. Cover and simmer for 10 minutes.
4. Add lime zest, lime juice and salt to the peaches and syrup mixture and refrigerate for at least 4 hours.
6. Remove refrigerated mixture and add to the Yonanas Healthy Dessert Maker®.
7. Press down with the plunger.
8. Enjoy!

Refreshing Raspberry Mango Sorbet

Try this cool and refreshing sorbet, filled with chunks of fruits like raspberries and mangos.

Serves: 8
Total Time: 45 minutes

INGREDIENTS:

3 cups frozen mango, cubed
1 cup frozen raspberries
1 cup full fat coconut milk, canned and chilled
1 cup of sugar
1 tsp lime juice
½ tsp salt

PREPARATION:

1. Combine milk, sugar, lime juice, and salt in a bowl and set aside.
2. Add 1 cup of the mango, ¼ cup of raspberries and a fourth of the milk mixture to your Yonanas Healthy Dessert Maker®.
3. Press down on the plunger.
4. Repeat steps 2 and 3 until all ingredients are used.
5. Enjoy.

Zesty Spicy Mango Sorbet

This 3-ingredient recipe packs a punch. If you seek something spicy look no further. Super simple, super spicy.

Serves: 2
Total Time: 5 minutes

INGREDIENTS:

1 cup mango, frozen and chopped
1 Tbsp. chili powder
¼ tsp lime zest

PREPARATION:

1. Combine ingredients.
2. Add mixture to your Yonanas Healthy Dessert Maker®.
3. Press down with the plunger when the chute gets full.
4. Enjoy!

Red, White and Blueberry Sorbet

Watermelon is incredibly healthy and hydrating. Blueberries are excellent sources of antioxidants. You can't go wrong with this simple sorbet.

Serves: 2
Total Time: 2 minutes

INGREDIENTS:

1 cup watermelon, chopped and frozen
¼ cup frozen blueberries

PREPARATION:

1. Combine ingredients.
2. Add mixture to your Yonanas Healthy Dessert Maker®.
3. Press down with the plunger when the chute gets full.
4. Enjoy!

Popsicles

Cool Blueberry Cheesecake Bites

Blueberry cheesecake makes everything right in the world, but no one really wants to spend the time and energy to actually make it. The preparation and laundry list of ingredients deters people from enjoying an awesome dessert. But now we have a 4-ingredient, 10-minute fix to blueberry cheesecake. No excuses. Make everything right again.

Serves: 4
Total Time: 10 minutes + 3 hours freeze time

INGREDIENTS:

4 Tbsp. sugar
2 cups Cool Whip®, frozen
2 cups frozen blueberries
½ cup cream cheese, sliced

PREPARATION:

1. Slice the cream cheese into squares and set aside.
2. Add some blueberries, a few spoonful of Cool Whip®, a tablespoon of sugar, and some slices of cream into your Yonanas Healthy Dessert Maker®.
3. Press down with the plunger.
4. Repeat steps 2 and 3 until all ingredients are used.
5. Spoon the mixture into popsicles trays or mini ice cube/candy molds and freeze for about 3 hours.
6. Enjoy!

Chocolate Banana Creamsicles

Tastes just almost just like the fudgesicles you find in the store, but healthier. No added sugar, just healthy ingredients full of real flavor.

Serves: 4
Total Time: 10 minutes
Cooking Time: 15 minutes +3 hours freeze time

INGREDIENTS:

4 Tbsp. cocoa powder
3 bananas, sliced and frozen
1 cup coconut milk, canned and chilled
1 tsp vanilla extract
¼ tsp salt

PREPARATION:

1. Combine coconut milk, vanilla extract, cocoa powder, and salt and set aside.
2. Add a third of the bananas and a third of the milk mixture to your Yonanas Healthy Dessert Maker®.
3. Press down with the plunger.
4. Repeat steps 2 and 3 until all ingredients are used.
5. Spoon mixture into popsicle trays and freeze for about 3 hours.
6. Enjoy.

CPBY Pops

Chocolate peanut butter yogurt pops. Enough said.

Serves: 8
Total Time: 10 minutes +4 hours freeze time

INGREDIENTS:

2 Tbsp. peanut butter
2 Tbsp. sweetened cocoa powder
1 ½ bananas, frozen and sliced
1 cup almond milk
1 Tbsp. honey
1 tsp vanilla extract
¾ cup plain non-fat Greek yogurt

PREPARATION:

1. Combine yogurt, vanilla, milk, honey, and cocoa powder. Set aside.
2. Add half the bananas, 1 Tbsp. peanut butter and half the yogurt mixture to the Yonanas Healthy Dessert Maker ®.
3. Press down on the plunger.
4. Repeat steps 2 and 3 until all ingredients are used.
5. Enjoy.

Luscious Pineapple Coconut Yogurt Pops

These silky-smooth pineapple and coconut popsicles with melt in your mouth. With double the pineapple and double the coconut, the flavor is one of a kind. Rich. Luscious. Silky smooth.

Serves: 4 - 5
Total Time: 5 minutes + 8 hours freeze time

INGREDIENTS:

2 containers (5.3oz.) non-fat pineapple yogurt
1 cup frozen pineapple chunks
1 cup coconut milk, canned and chilled
1 Tbsp. sugar
¾ tsp coconut extract

PREPARATION:

1. Mix extract, sugar, yogurt, and milk in a bowl and set aside.
2. Add half the pineapples and half the yogurt mixture to the Yonanas Healthy Dessert Maker ®.
3. Press down on the plunger.
4. Repeat steps 2 and 3.
5. Spoon mixture into popsicle trays and freeze for 8 hours.
5. Enjoy.

Chunky Minty Peach Pops

Bits of mint mixed with chunks of peaches and a hint of vanilla; this recipe is sure to awaken your senses.

Serves: 8-12
Total Time: 15 minutes + 2 hours freeze time

INGREDIENTS:

2 ½ cups frozen peaches, sliced
2 Tbsp. lemon juice
1 tsp fresh mint, chopped
¼ cup frozen orange juice concentrate
¼ cup sugar
¼ tsp vanilla extract

PREPARATION:

1. Pour the lemon juice and vanilla extract over the frozen peaches. Stir in the chopped mint and sugar.
2. Add half the peaches and half the concentrate to your Yonanas Healthy Dessert Maker®.
3. Press down on the plunger.
4 Repeat steps 2 and 3.
5. Spoon the mixture into popsicle trays and freeze for about 2 hours.
6. Enjoy!

Mega Mint Chocolate Chipsicles

What's a chipsicle you ask? A creamsicle with all the creamy goodness plus chopped up chocolate chips. An awesome hybrid.

Serves: 8-10
Total Time: 10 minutes + 6 hours freeze time

INGREDIENTS:

2 ½ cups vanilla almond milk
2 bananas, sliced and frozen
2 Tbsp. honey
1 tsp mint extract
1 cup semisweet chocolate chips

PREPARATION:

1. Mix the bananas and chocolate chips together in a bowl. Set aside.
2. Add the mint extract to the almond milk and set aside.
3. Add half the bananas, 1 tablespoon of honey and half the milk your Yonanas Healthy Dessert Maker®.
4. Press down with the plunger.
5. Repeat steps 3 and 4.
6. Transfer mixture to popsicle trays and freeze for 6 hours.

Chocolatey Raspberry Fro-Yo Pops

This mix of creamy yogurt, chocolate and raspberries makes for luscious and silky frozen yogurt pops. Enjoy anytime, morning or night.

Serves: 10
Total Time: 10 minutes +6 hours freeze time

INGREDIENTS:

4 Tbsp. sugar
2 cups frozen raspberries
2 cups plain Greek yogurt
½ cup chocolate chips

PREPARATION:

1. Mix sugar and yogurt in a bowl and set aside.
2. Add 1 cup of the raspberries, 1 cup of the yogurt mixture and ¼ cup of the chocolate chips in your Yonanas Healthy Dessert Maker®.
3. Press down with the plunger.
4. Repeat steps 2 and 3.
5. Spoon into popsicle trays and freeze for at least 6 hours.

Slice of Summer Watermelon Yogurt Pops

Summer can be possible at any time in your home with this very unique recipe for watermelon yogurt pops. Yep, that's right, watermelon and yogurt. Take the refreshing, juicy flavor of watermelon and marry it to the creamy texture of yogurt.

Serves: 8
Total Time: 10 minutes + 4 hours freeze time

INGREDIENTS:

3 cups frozen watermelon, cubed
1 Tbsp. lemon juice
½ cup Greek yogurt
¼ cup sugar

PREPARATION:

1. Combine lemon juice, yogurt and sugar in a bowl and set aside.
2. Alternate adding watermelon cubes and yogurt mixture to your Yonanas Healthy Dessert Maker®.
3. Continue to plunge when the chute gets full until all ingredients are used.
4. Spoon into popsicle trays and freeze for at least 4 hours.

Very Vanilla Pineapple Popsicles

Some people think vanilla is boring. Well, it's definitely not boring when we pair it with pineapple and turn it into a delicious, cold treat.

Serves: 4
Total Time: 5 minutes + 3 hours freeze time

INGREDIENTS:

2 cups of frozen pineapple chunks
½ tsp vanilla bean paste
¼ tsp salt

PREPARATION:

1. Add all ingredients to your Yonanas Healthy Dessert Maker®.
2. Press down on the plunger.
3. Spoon into popsicle trays and freeze for at least 3 hours.

Berry Swirl Popsicles

Red, white and blue. Layer or swirl. You choose. Who doesn't like a fun and colorful treat?

Serves: 10
Total Time: 5 minutes + 3 hours freeze time

INGREDIENTS:

2 cups vanilla yogurt
2 Tbsp. sugar
1 cup frozen raspberries
1 cup frozen blueberries

PREPARATION:

1. Mix sugar and yogurt in a small bowl.
2. Alternate adding yogurt, raspberries and blueberries your Yonanas Healthy Dessert Maker®.
3. Plunge when chute gets full. Continue until all ingredients are used.
4. Spoon into popsicles trays and freeze for 3 hours.

Piña Colada Paradise Popsicles

This 2-ingredient, sans-alcohol treat, is fun for the whole family! The only bummer is that little paper umbrellas can't fit in popsicles.

Serves: 6
Total Time: 5 minutes + 3 hours freeze time

INGREDIENTS:

2 ½ cups frozen pineapple chunks
1 can coconut milk, chilled

PREPARATION:

1. Toss everything into the Yonanas Healthy Dessert Maker®.
2. Press down on the plunger when full, until all ingredients are used.
3. Spoon into popsicle trays and freeze for at least 3 hours.

Zesty Stacked Raspberry Coconut Popsicles

This layered recipe allows you to enjoy the different flavors, tasting each separately, with the previous layer's flavor lingering long enough to tantalize your taste buds.

Serves: 7-9
Total Time: 25minutes +6 hours freeze time

INGREDIENTS:

5 Tbsp. lime juice
4 Tbsp. honey
2 Tbsp. stevia
2 tsp lime zest
1 ½ cups frozen raspberries
1 banana, sliced and frozen
1 can of coconut milk, chilled

PREPARATION:

1. Mix the coconut milk, 2 tablespoons of honey and 1 tablespoon of stevia in a small bowl. Set aside.
2. Pour a third of the coconut mixture into your popsicle trays and freeze for 15 minutes.
3. Mix remaining ingredients together in a large bowl and add them to the Yonanas Healthy Dessert Maker®.
4. Be sure to press down on the plunger if the chute gets full.
5. Remove popsicle trays and spoonthe mixture on top of the partially frozen coconut mixture.
6. Freeze for 6 hours.

Creamy Banana Nutella Fudgesicles

Nutella we love you. This recipe proves that love. These fudgesicles will rock your socks off. If you are already a Nutella fan, then you already know that there is no end to experimenting with the awesomeness that is Nutella, but if you've never tried this hazelnut chocolate butter, this is a great way to start your journey.

Serves: 6-10
Total Time: 5 minutes + 6 hours freeze time

INGREDIENTS:

4 bananas, sliced and frozen
½ cup Nutella
¼ cup plain yogurt

PREPARATION:

1. Mix the Nutella and yogurt together in a bowl.
2. Add ¼ of the bananas and ¼ of the yogurt mixture to your Yonanas Healthy Dessert Maker®.
3. Press down with the plunger.
4. Repeat steps 2 and 3 until all ingredients are used.
5. Spoon mixture into popsicles molds and freeze for 6 hours.
6. Enjoy.

Indulgent Strawberry Yogurt Pops

These two basic ingredients make a not so basic frozen treat. Strawberries and vanilla yogurt complement each other well, but this recipe takes it to a whole new category of treats by turning them into yogurt pops.

Serves: 4
Total Time: 3 minutes + 4 hours freeze time

INGREDIENTS:

1 cup frozen strawberries
½ cup vanilla yogurt

PREPARATION:

1. Run all the strawberries through your Yonanas Healthy Dessert Maker®, pressing down with the plunger when the chute is full.
2. Layer the strawberry mixture and yogurt in popsicles trays.
3. Freeze for 4 hours.

Mama's Mango Peach Pops

Tangy, succulent and frozen. This is all you need for some fruity frozen treats. Don't feel guilty, it's all natural.

Serves: 10
Total Time: 5 minutes + 3 hours freeze time

INGREDIENTS:

3 mangos, cubed and frozen
3 peaches, sliced and frozen
3 Tbsp. orange juice

PREPARATION:

1. Add 1/3 of the mangos, 1/3 of the peaches and 1 Tbsp. of orange juice into your Yonanas Healthy Dessert Maker®.
2. Press down with the plunger.
3. Repeat steps 1 and 2 until all ingredients are used.
4. Spoon into popsicles trays and freeze for about 3 hours.

Cakes and Pies

Choco Ban Ban Ice Cream Bites

This 2-ingredient recipe is a whole lot of bananas in every bite. No, really. Bananas and chocolate chips! That's it.

Serves: 24
Total Time: 3 hours

INGREDIENTS:

6 bananas, sliced and frozen
¾ cup mini chocolate chips

PREPARATION:

1. Alternate adding bananas and chocolate chips to your Yonanas Healthy Dessert Maker®.
2. Press down with the plunger when the chute gets full. Continue until all ingredients are used.
3. Spoon mixture into lightly greased mini muffin pans.
4. Freeze for 1 hour.
5. Pop out treats from the muffin tins using a butter knife. Store in a freezer bag or container.

Cake Batter Brilliance

Cake batter! Don't pretend you don't love it; we know you do. This vegan recipe allows for cake batter ice cream whenever you want. No eggs, no dairy, no gluten.

Serves: 4
Total Time: 5 minutes

INGREDIENTS:

5 bananas, sliced and frozen
2 Tbsp. agave nectar
2 Tbsp. sprinkles
2 Tbsp. vanilla extract
1 tsp butter extract
¼ tsp almond extract
¼ tsp maple extract
¼ tsp baking soda

PREPARATION:

1. Mix all the extracts, agave nectar, and baking soda together and set aside.
2. Alternate adding bananas and extract mixture through the Yonanas Healthy Dessert Maker®.
3. Press down with the plunger when the chute is full.
4. Repeat steps 2 and 3 until all ingredients are used.
5. Top with sprinkles.
6. Indulge.

Tart Chocolate Cherry Ice Cream Pie

Who knew the Yonanas Healthy Dessert Maker® could make pies? Impressive, right? We're impressed, you're impressed, and we are sure your friends will be impressed. It's super simple, and you only need 4 ingredients. So, get after it!

Serves: 8
Total Time: 15 minutes + 4 hours freeze time

INGREDIENTS:

4 Tbsp. chocolate chips
3 cups vanilla ice cream
1 ¼ cups frozen cherries, pitted
1 chocolate cookie pie crust (9 in.)

PREPARATION:

1. Mix the ice cream, 1 cup of cherries and 2 tablespoons of chocolate chips together in a bowl.
2. Spoon the mixture into your Yonanas Healthy Dessert Maker®.
3. Press down with the plunger when the chute gets full.
4. Repeat steps 2 and 3 until all ingredients are used.
5. Cut up the remaining cherries into small pieces.
6. Smooth mixture into pie crust. Top with remaining cherries and chocolate chips.
7. Freeze for about 4 hours.

Oh-My Mango Coconut Pie

Mango pie? Give it a try! It's different. Get a bunch of different textures. The crunchy goodness of the cookie crust, creamy layered inside and crispy toasted coconut topping.

Serves: 8
Total Time: 35 minutes + 4 hours freeze time

INGREDIENTS:

3 Tbsp. canola oil
2 cups gingersnap crumbs
2 Tbsp. toasted coconut
1 cup vanilla Greek yogurt
1 banana, sliced and frozen
1 mango, cubed and frozen
¾ cup heavy cream
¼ cup sugar
½ tsp coconut extract

PREPARATION:

1. Preheat oven to 350 degrees.
2. Lightly grease a 9-inch pie pan.
3. Mix the oil and gingersnap crumbs together.
4. Press the crumb mixture into the pie pan and bake for 10 minutes. Set aside to cool completely.
5. Use a hand mixer to mix the cream to thicken.
6. Slowly add the sugar and continue mixing until it forms peaks.
7. Add in the yogurt and coconut extract.
8. Run ½ the banana slices, ½ the mango and ½ the yogurt mixture through your Yonanas Healthy Dessert Maker®.
9. Press down with the plunger.
10. Repeat steps 8 and 9.
11. Pour the mixture into your completely cooled pie crust and garnish with toasted coconut pieces.
12. Freeze for at least 4 hours.

Daiquiri Pie

Daiquiris!!! A classic cocktail, but an even better frozen pie. Try it out and bring the Caribbean to you!

Serves: 8
Total Time: 25 minutes + 5 hours freeze time

INGREDIENTS:

3 Tbsp. canola oil
2 cups graham cracker crumbs
2 cups frozen strawberries
2 Tbsp. white rum
1 cup vanilla Greek yogurt
1 Tbsp. lime zest
¾ cup heavy cream
½ cup sugar

PREPARATION:

1. Preheat oven to 350 degrees.
2. Lightly grease a 9-inch pie pan and set aside.
3. Combine oil and graham cracker crumbs to make the pie crust. Press down in the pie pan.
3. Bake the crust for 10 minutes and then set aside to cool completely.
4. Use a hand mixer to whisk the cream until it thickens. Add in the sugar. Continue whisking until peaks form.
5. Gently stir yogurt, 2 tsp lime zest, and rum to the cream mixture.
6. Alternate adding 1 cup of strawberries and cream mixture to the Yonanas Healthy Dessert Maker®.
7. Press down with the plunger when the chute gets full.
8. Repeat steps 6 and 7 until all ingredients are used.
9. Pour mixture into the completely cooled pie crust.
8. Garnish with remaining strawberries and lime zest.
9. Freeze for 5 hours.

Blackberry Lemon Drop Ice Cream Pie

Tart. Crisp. Refreshing. Zesty. Tangy. With a hint of sugary sweetness. That is this ice cream pie.

Serves: 8
Total Time: 30 minutes + 5 hours freeze time

INGREDIENTS:

3 Tbsp. canola oil
3 cups frozen blackberries
2 cups gingersnap cookie crumbs
2 tsp lemon zest
1 cup vanilla Greek yogurt
¾ cup heavy cream
½ cup sugar

PREPARATION:

1. Preheat oven to 350 degrees.
2. Lightly grease a 9-inch pie pan.
3. Combine oil and cookie crumbs. Press into pie pan to create the crust.
4. Whisk cream with a hand mixer until it thickens. Add in sugar and continue whisking until peaks form.
5. Add yogurt and zest to the cream mixture.
3. Alternate adding 2 cups of the blackberries and cream mixture to your Yonanas Healthy Dessert Maker® until all ingredients are used, pressing down with the plunger when the chute gets full.
4. Pour the mixture into the completely cooled crust and garnish with remaining blackberries.
5. Freeze for 5 hours.

Fantastic Frozen Raspberry Pie

So we get it. Frozen pies take a little bit longer to make and are more involved than the typical Yonanas recipe, but this one is well worth the extra trouble. Full of raspberries and chocolate you can't go wrong. Luscious. Silky. Just like the frozen pies from the freezer section.

Serves: 8
Total Time: 45 minutes + 5 hours freeze time

INGREDIENTS:

33 chocolate wafer crumbs
cups frozen raspberries
3 tbsp. canola oil
2 tbsp. lemon juice
2 large egg whites, room temperature
2 tbsp. milk
1 tbsp. butter
¾ cup sugar
½ cup cream of tartar
¼ tsp salt

PREPARATION:

1. Preheat oven to 350 degrees.
2. Lightly grease a 9-inch pie pan.
3. Combine wafer crumbs, oil, milk, butter, and ¼ cup sugar to create the pie crust.
4. Press the crust mixture into the pie pan and bake for 12 minutes. Set aside to cool completely.
5. Pour lemon juice and salt over the raspberries.
6. Add raspberries to your Yonanas Healthy Dessert Maker®, pressing down with the plunger when the chute gets full.
7. Simmer about 1 inch of water in a large skillet or saucepan.
8. Using a hand mixer, combine egg whites, remaining sugar and cream of tartar in a stainless-steel bowl. Mix on medium speed until foamy.
9. Hold the bowl over the simmering water and mix on medium speed for another 3 ½ minutes until the mixture turns thick and glossy.

10. Continue mixing, but increase the speed to high. Mix for another 3 ½ minutes, still over the saucepan, until the mixture because very thick.

11. Remove the bowl from over the simmering water and continue to mix for about 4 minutes on medium speed until the mixture cools to room temperature.

12. Combine the egg mixture with the raspberry mixture and spread into the pie crust.

13. Garnish with remaining cookie crumbs.

14. Freeze for 5 hours.

Terrific Raspberry and Chocolate Terrine

Raspberry chocolate terrine. Layers of raspberry, chocolate, and yogurt. A classic dessert loaf made within minutes.

Serves: 8
Total Time: 10 minutes + 3 hours freeze time

INGREDIENTS:

4 cups vanilla yogurt
2 tbsp. sweetened cocoa powder
1 ½ cups frozen raspberries

PREPARATION:

1. Take and 8 x 4 pan and line it with plastic wrap.
2. Mix 2 cups of yogurt and cocoa powder in a bowl and set aside.
3. Run the remaining 2 cups of yogurt and raspberries through your Yonanas Healthy Dessert Maker®, pressing down on the plunger when the chute gets full.
4. Pour half of the raspberry mixture into the pan. Spread the chocolate mixture on top, and then finish with a layer of the remaining raspberry mixture.
5. Freeze for at least 5 hours.

Frozen Classic Pineapple Upside Down Cake

Many moons ago cakes were made in cast iron skillets. The fruit was at the bottom, and the cake was cooked on top. We have morphed this old-time dessert many times and have finally perfected it into a frozen dessert.

Serves: 8
Total Time: 5 minutes

INGREDIENTS:

20 oz. bag of frozen pineapple rings
7 oz. angel food cake
6 tbsp. light brown sugar
5 frozen cherries, pitted
3 large egg yolks, room temperature
2 large egg whites, room temperature
½ cup sugar
½ cup heavy cream
½ tsp cream of tartar

PREPARATION:

1. Lightly grease a 9-inch spring form pan.
2. Place 5 pineapple rings on the bottom of the spring form pan and put one cherry in the middle of each ring.
3. Chop the remaining pineapple rings into chunks and run through your Yonanas Healthy Dessert Maker®, plunging when the chute gets full.
4. Using a hand mixer, mix the egg yolks and brown sugar in a stainless-steel bowl for about 3 minutes until the mixture turns fluffy.
5. Beat in the pineapple mixture.
6. Simmer 1 inch of water in a large saucepan.
7. Mix the pineapple mixture on medium speed over the simmering water for about 7 minutes or until it gets thick and doubled in volume.
8. Remove the mixture from above the water and beat for another 8 minutes until it reaches room temperature.

9. Rinse and dry the beaters or get another set of clean ones.

10. Mix the egg whites, sugar and cream of tartar on medium speed in a stainless-steel bowl for about 3 minutes or until it turns foamy.

11. Continue to mix over the simmering water for about 3 minutes or until it becomes slightly glossy.

12. Increase the mixer speed and continue to beat for another 5 minutes or until the mixture turns thick.

13. Remove from above the water and reduce hand mixer speed to medium for another 5 minutes until the mixture reaches room temperature.

14. Combine with the pineapple mixture.

15. Using another set of beaters, or cleaning the ones you have once again, mix the cream for about 1 minute or until it forms soft peaks.

16. Gently mix the cream and batter together.

17. Pour into the spring form pan with the pineapple slices and cherries.

18. Cut 9 slices of angel food cake and place them over the batter.

19. Freeze for 8 hours.

20. Pat yourself on the back for a job well done on this experienced level recipe. You are now a Yonanas Healthy Dessert Maker® expert chef.

Very Berry Oreo Pie

Have an Oreo craving? Feel less guilty by jazzing it up with some frozen fruit. That's what the Yonanas Healthy Dessert Maker® is all about right? Healthier choices.

Serves: 8
Total Time: 20 minutes + 4 hours freeze time

INGREDIENTS:

34 Oreo cookies, crumbled
4 bananas, sliced and frozen
3 tbsp. canola oil
1 ½ cups frozen mixed berries

PREPARATION:

1. Combine Oreo crumbs and oil.
2. Press into a 9-inch pie pan creating the crust. Set aside.
3. Add ¼ of the bananas and ¼ of the frozen berries to you Yonanas Healthy Dessert Maker®.
4. Press down with the plunger.
5. Repeat steps 3 and 4 until all ingredients are used.
6. Transfer fruit mixture to the Oreo crust.
7. Freeze for at least 4 hours.

Crazy Cool Cranberry and Orange Frozen Pie

Sugar and spice and everything nice. Minus the sugar. Try this cranberry orange recipe for a scrumptious frozen pie.

Serves: 8
Total Time: 25 minutes + 4 hours freeze time

INGREDIENTS:

4 bananas, sliced and frozen
3 tbsp. canola oil
2 cups graham cracker crumbs
2 tsp cinnamon
2 tsp orange zest
1 cup frozen cranberries

PREPARATION:

1. Preheat oven to 350 degrees.
2. Lightly grease a 9-inch pie pan.
3. Combine graham cracker crumbs, cinnamon and canola oil to create the crust. Press into pie pan.
4. Bake the crust for 10 minutes. Set aside to cool completely.
5. Run ¼ of the bananas, ¼ of the cranberries and ¼ of the zest through your Yonanas Healthy Dessert Maker®.
6. Press down with the plunger.
7. Repeat steps 5 and 6 until all ingredients are used.
8. Spoon fruit mixture into completely cooled pie crust.
9. Freeze for 4 hours.

Simple and Sweet Strawberry Shortcake

Just like mom used to make, this strawberry shortcake hits all the stops. Juicy and spongy. Just perfect.

Serves: 2
Total Time: 10 minutes

INGREDIENTS:

4 bananas, sliced and frozen
3 cup frozen strawberries
2 shortcake dessert cups

PREPARATION:

1. Run the bananas and 2 ½ cups of the frozen strawberries through your Yonanas Healthy Dessert Maker®, pressing down with the plunger when the chute gets full, until all ingredients are used.
2. Spoon fruit mixture into dessert cups.
3. Garnish with remaining strawberries and their juices.
4. Enjoy immediately.

Sweet and Sour Blueberry Lemon Trifle

You will be hard pressed to find a better topping for pound cake than blueberry and lemon ice cream. We combine all the necessary ingredients for a delicious dessert in this oh so tasty trifle. You get different textures and tastes with an explosion of flavor.

Serves: 2
Total Time: 5 minutes

INGREDIENTS:

4 bananas, sliced and frozen
1 cup frozen blueberries
1 tbsp. lemon zest
1 sliced of pound cake
½ cup fresh blueberries

PREPARATION:

1. Run ½ the bananas through the Yonanas Healthy Dessert Maker® and set aside.
2. Run the remaining bananas, frozen blueberries, and lemon zest through the machine. Set aside.
3. Place ½ a slice of pound cake at the bottom of your trifle dish.
4. Put ½ of the fresh blueberries on top of the pound cake.
5. Add a layer of the banana Yonanas.
6. Place the other ½ of the pound cake on top of the bananas.
7. Spread the lemon and blueberry Yonanas on top of the pound cake layer.
8. Top with the remaining fresh blueberries.
9. Enjoy!

Healthy Desserts

Vegan Oatmeal Raisin Cookie Dough Ice Cream

Cookie dough ice cream your favorite? Of course. Your Yonanas Healthy Dessert Maker® can do that too!

Serves: 2
Total Time: 10 minutes

INGREDIENTS:

2 bananas, sliced and frozen
2 tbsp. vanilla almond milk
½ tsp cinnamon
¼ cup raisins
¼ cup raw oatmeal

PREPARATION:

1. Combine cinnamon, bananas, and milk.
2. Combine raisins and oatmeal.
3. Add half the bananas and half the oatmeal mixture to your Yonanas Healthy Dessert Maker ®.
4. Press down on the plunger.
5. Repeat steps 3 and 4.
6. Enjoy.

Creamy Chocolatey Banana Ice Cream

Try out some almond butter and almond milk in this delicious chocolatey recipe. Chocolate chips add a nice crunchy texture to this ice cream as well. Double chocolate? Yes, please.

Serves: 2
Total Time: 10 minutes

INGREDIENTS:

3 bananas, sliced and frozen
1 tbsp. almond butter
½ tbsp. cocoa powder
½ cup mini chocolate chips
¼ cup almond milk

PREPARATION:

1. Combine almond milk and cocoa powder. Set aside.
2. Alternate adding bananas, milk, butter, and chocolate chips to your Yonanas Healthy Dessert Maker®.
3. Press down with the plunger when the chute gets full.
4. Repeat steps 2 and 3 until all ingredients are used.
5. Enjoy.

Pineapple Whipped Cream

This is not your average whipped cream. It's sugar-free and frozen! Oh, and did we mention pineapple flavored? You're welcome.

Serves: 1
Total Time: 10 minutes

INGREDIENTS:

2 cups frozen pineapple chunks
2 tbsp. coconut milk
1 banana, sliced and frozen

PREPARATION:

1. Alternate adding pineapple, milk, and bananas to your Yonanas Healthy Dessert Maker®.
2. Press down with the plunger when the chute gets full.
3. Repeat steps 1 and 2 until all ingredients are used.
4. Enjoy.

Jamie's Java Ice Cream

Another great excuse to have ice cream for breakfast! And chocolate ice cream at that. Get your morning fix of all things good with this espresso ice cream.

Serves: 3
Total Time: 10 minutes

INGREDIENTS:

4 bananas, sliced and frozen
2 tbsp. sweetened cocoa powder
1 tsp instant espresso
¼ cup chocolate chips

PREPARATION:

1. Combine espresso and cocoa powder.
2. Pour over the bananas.
3. Add ½ the bananas and ½ the chocolate chips to your Yonanas Healthy Dessert Maker®.
4. Press down with the plunger when the chute gets full.
5. Repeat steps 3 and 4 until all ingredients are used.
6. Enjoy.

Instant Banana Nut Chip Ice Cream

This recipe tastes just like banana nut bread...just cold and without the bread. Reason enough to try it, right?

Serves: 2
Total Time: 10 minutes

INGREDIENTS:

3 bananas, sliced and frozen
1 tbsp. maple syrup
½ tsp cinnamon
½ cup toasted walnuts, chopped
½ cup chocolate chips

PREPARATION:

1. Combine walnuts and chocolate chips. Set aside.
2. Sprinkle cinnamon on top of the bananas.
3. Alternate adding all ingredients to the Yonanas Healthy Dessert Maker®.
4. Press down with the plunger when the chute gets full.
5. Repeat steps 3 and 4 until all ingredients are used.
6. Enjoy.

Passion Peach Ice Cream

When have you tried an ice cream with bananas, watermelon, and peaches? Never, right? Well, let's change that. This mix it magical. Your taste buds will thank you.

Serves: 4
Total Time: 5 minutes

INGREDIENTS:

2 bananas, sliced and frozen
2 cups frozen watermelon chunks
2 cups frozen peaches, sliced

PREPARATION:

1. Add ½ the bananas, 1 cup of the watermelon chunks and 1 cup of the sliced peaches to your Yonanas Healthy Dessert Maker®.
2. Press down with the plunger when the chute gets full.
3. Repeat steps 1 and 2 until all ingredients are used.
4. Enjoy.

Bodacious Berrylicious

Banana is the main flavor here, but expect explosions of berry. The small amounts of raspberries, blueberries, and cranberries help to add little bursts of berry flavor.

Serves: 2
Total Time: 5 minutes

INGREDIENTS:

2 bananas, sliced and frozen
1 tbsp. frozen raspberries
1 tbsp. frozen blueberries
1 tbsp. cranberries

PREPARATION:

1. Alternate adding ingredients to your Yonanas Healthy Dessert Maker®.
2. Press down on the plunger when the chute gets full.
3. Repeat steps 1 and 2 until all ingredients are used.
4. Enjoy.

Cherry Almond Nice Cream

Be nice to yourself. Indulge in this rich cherry almond ice cream. Not to worry, it is sugar and low-cal.

Serves: 2
Total Time: 5 minutes

INGREDIENTS:

2 bananas, sliced and frozen
2 cups frozen cherries, pitted
½ tsp almond extract

PREPARATION:

1. Combine bananas and cherries. Pour extract on top.
2. Feed fruit mixture through your Yonanas Healthy Dessert Maker®, pressing down with the plunger when the chute gets full.
3. Guiltlessly indulge. Share if you must.

Ooey Gooey S'mores Ice Cream

S'mores are usually served in cold weather while warming by the fire. Let's flip the script! Eat some ice-cold s'mores on a warm day.

Serves: 2
Preparation Time: 40 minutes
Cooking Time: 20 minutes

INGREDIENTS:

10 mini marshmallows
2 bananas, sliced and frozen
2 tbsp. mini chocolate chips
1 graham cracker, crumbled

PREPARATION:

1. Toast the marshmallows in a skillet over medium heat or with a small kitchen torch.
2. Run the bananas through your Yonanas Healthy Dessert Maker®, pressing down with the plunger when the chute is full.
3. Hand mix the graham cracker crumbs, chocolate bits, and marshmallows into the banana ice cream.
4. Enjoy.

Decadent Dark Chocolate PB Bananas Ice Cream

A dark chocolate fan? Ask, and you shall receive. This ice cream is chock-full of dark chocolate and peanut butter with just a hint of cinnamon.

Serves: 2
Total Time: 10 minutes

INGREDIENTS:

4 bananas, sliced and frozen
2 tbsp. dark chocolate chips
2 tbsp. dark chocolate cocoa powder
2 tbsp. peanut butter
½ tsp cinnamon
¼ tsp salt

PREPARATION:

1. Mix cocoa powder, salt, and cinnamon. Sprinkle over bananas.
2. Alternate adding ingredients to your Yonanas Healthy Dessert Maker®.
3. Press down on the plunger when the chute gets full.
4. Enjoy.

Non-Dessert Recipes

Mom's Mashed Potatoes Made Easy

Fluffy, buttery, perfect mashed potatoes just like Mom used to make. Treat yourself to a homemade treat.

Serves: 6
Total Time: 20 minutes

INGREDIENTS:

4 Russet potatoes, peeled and chopped
1 stick of butter
1 cup cream cheese, cut into squares
1 cup sour cream
½ tsp salt
¼ cup heavy cream
¼ cup parmesan cheese, grated

PREPARATION:

1. Boil the potatoes for about 15 minutes or until soft.
2. Drain the potatoes and combine all ingredients.
3. Run entire mixture to your Yonanas Healthy Dessert Maker® pressing down with the plunger when the chute gets full.
4. Enjoy.

Cinnamon Mashed Sweet Potatoes

Warm your heart, soul and all your insides with these sweet cinnamon mashed potatoes. Just enough sweet, just enough spice and everything's nice.

Serves: 2
Total Time: 5 minutes

INGREDIENTS:

2 sweet potatoes, peeled and chopped
2 tbsp. brown sugar
1 tbsp. cinnamon
½ cup milk

PREPARATION:

1. Boil potatoes for about 15 minutes or until they soften.
2. Drain the potatoes.
3. Combine all ingredients.
4. Run all ingredients through your Yonanas Healthy Dessert Maker® plunging when the chute gets full.
5. Enjoy.

Garlicy Sweet Potato Magic

Take sweet potatoes to a not so sweet level. Add some garlic for a new and exciting kick to mashed sweet potatoes.

Serves: 5
Total Time: 20 minutes

INGREDIENTS:

4 sweet potatoes, peeled and chopped
2 tbsps. sour cream
2 garlic cloves, chopped
1 tbsp. butter
1 tsp salt
1 tsp pepper
½ cup milk

PREPARATION:

1. Boil the potatoes about 15 minutes or until soft.
2. Drain the potatoes.
3. Combine all ingredients.
4. Add ingredients to your Yonanas Healthy Dessert Maker® pressing down with the plunger when the chute gets full.
5. Enjoy.

Ranch Dream Mashed Potatoes

Ranch makes everything better. The spicy zing dresses up these mashed potatoes and makes a delicious side dish for any meal.

Serves: 6
Total Time: 20 minutes

INGREDIENTS:

3 garlic cloves, chopped
2 lbs. red potatoes
2 tbsps. butter
2 tbsps. chives, chopped
1 package Ranch dressing mix
¼ cup heavy cream

PREPARATION:

1. Boil potatoes for 15 minutes, or until soft.
2. Drain potatoes.
3. Combine all ingredients.
4. Run all ingredients through your Yonanas Healthy Dessert Maker®.
5. Press down with the plunger when the chute gets full.
6. Enjoy.

McCreamy Whipped Parsnips

Mayonnaise leaves these sharp-tasting root vegetable creamy and full of flavor. Impress your friends with this unique recipe.

Serves: 4
Total Time: 20 minutes

INGREDIENTS:

2 tbsps. butter
2 tbsps. mayonnaise
2 garlic cloves, chopped
1 lb. parsnips, peeled and chopped
1 tsp salt
1 tsp pepper

PREPARATION:

1. Boil the parsnips for about 15 minutes or until soft.
2. Drain.
3. Combine all ingredients.
4. Run mixture through your Yonanas Healthy Dessert Maker® pressing down on the plunger when the chute gets full.
5. Enjoy.

I Can't Believe It's Not Pumpkin Butter

Add some sweetness to your life with this delectable pumpkin butter recipe. Try it on your favorite carbs like potatoes, bagels, and toast. Yum, yum.

Yields: 1.5 cups
Total Time: 5 minutes

INGREDIENTS:

1 cup butter, softened
1 tbsp. honey
1 tsp cinnamon
¼ cup pumpkin puree
¼ cup powdered sugar
¼ cup nutmeg
¼ tsp ground cloves

PREPARATION:

1. Combine all ingredients.
2. Run the mixture through your Yonanas Healthy Dessert Maker®.
3. Press down with the plunger when the chute gets full.
4. Store covered in an airtight container until ready to use.

Rich Rosemary and Roasted Garlic Butter

Butter makes everything better, but jazz it up this time around with some rosemary and garlic. Best part? No churning necessary.

Yields: ½ cup
Total Time: 50 minutes

INGREDIENTS:

2 tbsps. rosemary, chopped
1 head of garlic, trimmed ¼ in from the top
1 tsp oil
1 stick of butter, softened
¼ tsp salt

PREPARATION:

1. Preheat oven to 425 degrees.
2. Dollop oil on the garlic.
3. Wrap in foil and bake for 45 minutes.
4. Combine all ingredients.
5. Run through your Yonanas Healthy Dessert Maker®.
6. Store in an airtight container until ready to use.

Roasted Red Pepper and Feta Football Sunday Spread

Don't be basic with your cheese dips. Take a few minutes to mix things up with the fancy pants, sure to impress your friends, feta cheese spread.

Yields: 2 cups
Total Time: 5 minutes

INGREDIENTS:

2 tbsps. lime juice
1 cup feta cheese
1 garlic clove, minced
1 jalapeño
½ cup cream cheese
½ cup roasted red peppers
¼ tsp oregano
¼ tsp cumin
¼ cup cilantro
¼ cup mayonnaise
¼ cup sour cream

PREPARATION:

1. Combine all ingredients.
2. Run mixture through your Yonanas Healthy Dessert Maker® pressing down on the plunger when the chute is full.
3. Enjoy at room temperature or chill if desired.

Green Goddess Guac

No need to buy store bought guacamole anymore. This recipe is super-fast and easy. The cleanup easy and fast too!

Serves: 4
Total Time: 5 minutes

INGREDIENTS:

4 avocados
4 garlic cloves, minced
1 lime, juiced
¼ cup cilantro
¼ tsp salt
¼ tsp pepper

PREPARATION:

1. Combine all ingredients.
2. Add all ingredients to your Yonanas Healthy Dessert Maker®.
3. Press down with the plunger when the chute gets full.
4. Enjoy.

Cool Creamy Guacamole

Guacamole has never been this creamy. Silky smooth, and ready in an instant. Bring the party to your kitchen.

Serves: 4-6
Total Time: 5 minutes

INGREDIENTS:

3 avocados
1 jalapeño
1 tsp lemon juice
1 garlic cloves, minced
⅓ cup tomato, chopped
⅓ sour cream
⅓ red onion chopped
¼ tsp salt
¼ tsp pepper

PREPARATION:

1. Combine all ingredients.
2. Add mixture to your Yonanas Healthy Dessert Maker®.
3. Press down with the plunger when the chute gets full.
4. Enjoy.

White Bean Avocado Dip

Steer clear of everyday treats with this white bean and avocado dip. The avocados add a creamy texture to what was once a basic bean dip. Indulge.

Serves: 2
Total Time: 5 minutes

INGREDIENTS:

2 garlic cloves, minced
2 tbsps. extra virgin olive oil
2 tbsps. lime juice
2 tbsps. cilantro
1 can cannellini beans
½ avocado
½ jalapeño
½ cup spinach
¼ tsp salt
¼ tsp pepper

PREPARATION:

1. Combine all ingredients.
2. Add mixture to your Yonanas Healthy Dessert Maker®.
3. Press down with the plunger when the chute gets full.
4. Enjoy.

Rosemary, White Beans and Garlic Dip, OH MY!

Yonanas your way into a healthy and universal dip. This spread can be used on breads, sandwiches, cheeses, or as a dip for chips and veggies too!

Serves: 2
Total Time: 5 minutes

INGREDIENTS:

3 cans of white beans
3 garlic cloves, minced
1 ½ tsp rosemary, chopped
½ tsp salt
½ tsp pepper
½ lemon zest

PREPARATION:

1. Drain the white beans and set the liquid aside.
2. Combine all ingredients.
3. Add ingredients to your Yonanas Healthy Dessert Maker®.
4. Press down on the plunger when the chute gets full.
5. Stir in remaining liquid from the beans until you reach your desired consistency.
6. Enjoy

Not Your Basic Black Bean Dip

Simple recipe with complex flavor. The cumin in this recipe adds the perfect amount of flavor. Easy to make and everything but basic.

Yields: 3 cups
Total Time: 5 minutes

INGREDIENTS:

3 garlic cloves, minced
2 tsp lime juice
2 cans black beans, drained
1 tsp cumin
¾ cup salsa
¼ cup cilantro
¼ tsp salt

PREPARATION:

1. Combine all ingredients.
2. Add the mixture to your Yonanas Healthy Dessert Maker®.
3. Press down on the plunger when the chute gets full.
4. Enjoy.

Heavenly Hummus

Hummus goes with everything. No need for a special occasion or meal. Toss this tasty hummus on a burger or dip your veggies in it. Always keep it on hand for a spur of the moment snack idea.

Serves: 2
Total Time: 5 minutes

INGREDIENTS:

2 tbsps. lemon juice
2 tbsps. extra virgin olive oil
1 garlic clove, minced
¼ cup tahini

PREPARATION:

1. Combine all ingredients.
2. Add the mixture to your Yonanas Healthy Dessert Maker®.
3. Press down with the plunger when the chute gets full.
4. Enjoy immediately or save for spontaneous snacking.

1-2-3 Bush's Brand Hummus

Hummus has never been so easy. With Bush's new hummus packet and your Yonanas Healthy Dessert Maker® get creamy, authentic hummus in minutes.

Serves: 4
Total Time: 5 minutes

INGREDIENTS:

1 can garbanzo beans, drained
1 Bush's Classic Hummus Made Easy® packet

PREPARATION:

1. Combine both ingredients.
2. Add the mixture to your Yonanas Healthy Dessert Maker®.
3. Press down with the plunger when the chute gets full.
4. You're done! Enjoy.

Roasted Toasted Red Pepper Hummus

Dress up your hummus and do it all from scratch. Get the tangy taste of red pepper mixed with the creamy texture of hummus, and you're set.

Serves: 2
Total Time: 5 minutes

INGREDIENTS:

2 garlic cloves, minced
1 can garbanzo beans, drained
½ cup roasted red peppers
⅓ cup tahini
⅓ cup lemon juice
¼ tsp basil, dried

PREPARATION:

1. Combine ingredients.
2. Add mixture to your Yonanas Healthy Dessert Maker®.
3. Press down with the plunger when the chute gets full.
4. Enjoy!

1-2-3 Bush's Brand Red Pepper Hummus

Bush's makes a red pepper hummus mix that makes hummus as easy as ever. Everything is one little bag. Just pop everything into the Yonanas Healthy Dessert Maker® and you've got creamy red pepper goodness.

Serves: 2
Total Time: 5 minutes

INGREDIENTS:

1 can garbanzo beans, drained
1 packet Bush's Hummus Made Easy® Roasted Red Pepper

PREPARATION:

1. Combine both ingredients.
2. Add the mixture to your Yonanas Healthy Dessert Maker®.
3. Press down with the plunger when the chute gets full.
4. Enjoy.

Alcoholic Treats

Tasty Tiramisu

Turn tiramisu into a luscious alcoholic treat! You'll be sure to never eat this sweet Italian treat the traditional way ever again.

Serves: 2
Total Time: 5 minutes

INGREDIENTS:

2 bananas, frozen and sliced
2 tsp sweetened cocoa powder
1 lady finger
1 tsp dark chocolate chips or shavings
1 oz. coffee liqueur
½ tsp cinnamon

PREPARATION:

1. Sprinkle the cinnamon and cocoa powder over the banana slices.
2. Add the bananas to your Yonanas Healthy Dessert Maker®.
3. Press down with the plunger when the chute gets full.
4. Put the lady finger in your bow of Yonanas.
5. Pour the shot of liqueur on top.
6. Garnish with the dark chocolate.

Boozey Oreo Blast

The only thing that could possibly make Oreo cookie better is a shot of something boozy. Get the real cookies and cream flavor with this crunchy yet creamy concoction.

Serves: 2
Total Time: 5 minutes

INGREDIENTS:

4 Oreo cookies, crumbled
2 healthy scoops of vanilla ice cream
1 oz. Bailey's
1 oz. Disaronno
½ tsp milk

PREPARATION:

1. Combine Bailey's, Disaronno, cookie crumbs, and milk.
2. Alternate adding the mixture and vanilla ice cream your Yonanas Healthy Dessert Maker®.
3. Press down with the plunger when the chute gets full.
4. Enjoy!

Bailey's Frozen Yogurt Blast

Dress up your hummus and do it all from scratch. Get the tangy taste of red pepper mixed with the creamy texture of hummus, and you're set.

Serves: 2
Total Time: 5 minutes

INGREDIENTS:

2 tbsps. Bailey's
1 cup mini chocolate chips
1 ½ cups Cool Whip
½ cup sugar
¼ cup espresso
¼ cup water

PREPARATION:

1.Heat the espresso, water, and sugar on the stove until the sugar is dissolved. Set aside to cool
2. Mix the Bailey's and cooled espresso mixture.
3. Alternate adding heaping spoonfuls of Cool Whip, chocolate chips, and liquid to the Yonanas Healthy Dessert Maker®.
4. Press down with the plunger when the chute gets full.
5. Enjoy!

Mojito Madness

Everyone's loves a refreshing, minty mojito every now and then. Mojitos can get real awesome when you add run soaked bananas. Try out this intensely flavored cocktail.

Serves: 2
Total Time: 5 minutes +1-hour freeze time

INGREDIENTS:

2 bananas, sliced
2 tbsps. mint leaves
1 oz. lemon-lime seltzer water
1 tsp lime zest
½ frozen lime, cut into segments
¼ cup rum

PREPARATION:

1. Combine bananas, mint, and rum in a plastic bag. Freeze for one hour.
2. Add bananas, lime segments, and lime zest to your Yonanas Healthy Dessert Maker®.
3. Press down with the plunger when the chute gets full.
4. Pour the seltzer water over the Yonanas treat and enjoy!

Elegant Strawberries and Champagne Ice Cream

Strawberries and champagne make almost any girl's heart sing. Try this super easy that's sure to impress.

Serves: 2
Total Time: 5 minutes + 8 hours freeze time

INGREDIENTS:

2 bananas, sliced and frozen
2 cubes of frozen champagne
1 cup frozen strawberries

PREPARATION:

1. Freeze champagne in ice cube trays for 8 hours.
2. Add ½ of the bananas, 1 cube of champagne, and a ½ cup of strawberries to your Yonanas Healthy Dessert Maker®.
3. Press down with the plunger when the chute gets full.
4. Repeat steps 2 and 3.
5. Enjoy!

An Old Fashion Treat

Keep it classy and classic with this fresh twist on the well-known Old Fashion cocktail. Chocolate, cherries, orange, and bourbon. You can't go wrong marrying these flavors.

Serves: 2
Total Time: 5 minutes + 8 hours freeze time

INGREDIENTS:

2 bananas, sliced
1 oz. dark chocolate chips
¾ cup frozen cherries, pitted
½ tsp orange zest
¼ cup frozen oranges, cut into segments
¼ cup bourbon

PREPARATION:

1. Combine bananas and bourbon and freeze for 8 hours.
2. Add all ingredients to your Yonanas Healthy Dessert Maker®.
3. Press down with the plunger when the chute gets full.
4. Enjoy!

Simply Slammin' Sangria

Add a twist to traditional sangria and try it with a spoon! This ice cream cocktail is super simple, but don't be fooled, it still packs a punch.

Serves: 2
Total Time: 5 minutes

INGREDIENTS:

2 bananas, sliced and frozen
1 cup frozen mixed berries
¼ cup red wine
¼ cup frozen mixed berries with their juice

PREPARATION:

1. Combine bananas and 1 cup frozen mixed berries.
2. Add mixture to your Yonanas Healthy Dessert Maker®.
3. Press down with the plunger when the chute gets full.
4. Pour the wine and ¼ cup of mixed berries and juice on top of your frozen treat.
5. Enjoy.

Tart and Tangy Tequila Sunrise

We love our tequila anyway we can get it, but this recipe delivers on many counts. Unique? Check. Cold and refreshing? Check. Healthy dose of tequila? Check. Check. Check it out.

Serves: 2
Total Time: 5 minutes + 8 hours freeze time

INGREDIENTS:

2 bananas, sliced and frozen
¾ cup frozen cherries, pitted
½ tsp lime zest
¼ cup oranges, cut into segments
1.4 cup tequila

PREPARATION:

1. Add oranges and tequila in a plastic baggie. Freeze for 8 hours.
2. Combine all ingredients.
3. Add mixture to your Yonanas Healthy Dessert Maker®.
4. Press down with the plunger when the chute gets full.
5. Enjoy!

Join Our FREE Cookbook Club

Why should you join?

- ⊘ Get new books we publish for free
- ⊘ Get huge discounts on new products we promote
- ⊘ Get recipes, secrets and techniques straight from the pros to your inbox
- ⊘ Get access to our convenient kitchen guides

SIGN UP AT COOKINGWITHAFOODIE.COM

Made in the USA
Las Vegas, NV
08 February 2021

17510741R00085